From the Editor
2018

Pacific Daily Times Editorials

Jesse Steele

Amazon Paperback Edition

books.jessesteele.com

books@jessesteele.com

ISBN 978-1795780971

For MBI

Table of Contents

2019 Preface   iii

Editor Notes   xi

Articles by Date: 2018   1

About the Author   240

2019 Preface

My uncle used to warn me about China. For the record, he wasn't technically my *uncle*. Being my mother's cousin, he was my *first cousin once removed*. I say this to be factual and, so as not to digress, I shall simply call him my "uncle".

As I said, he used to warn me about China, long before I ever moved to Asia. This was twenty, even thirty years ago.

"China is a racist people," he would say. He never balanced his words with disclaimers because, being family, we all understood that he wasn't speaking about every single Chinese person in the world, but rather the thought that guided the nation of China today.

"In their mind, we are all less than human. They believe they are better than everyone else. And, they dream of a world where everyone is ethnically Chinese—the Chinese race. They won't stop until all other ethnicities are expunged and every country has only Han people with their Mandarin language. They are worse than the Nazis ever were and they are more determined."

Though I did not believe his words at face value, I did not forget them either. At the time, I just listened. I wasn't sure whether to believe him. He lacked proof, though he was a well-read, literate man, with even better command of the English language than my own mother and father.

Yes, I grew up in a family that used a large vocabulary. Yes, that probably contributed greatly to my own success in life. And yes, I'm getting a little off track, but not entirely.

While the words I just quoted are a paraphrase from my memories going back to my mid twenties, even early childhood, I grew up in a family that knew what words meant and how to use them. We knew how to learn about the world and how to explain what we learned.

So, I knew that clarity needed two things: I needed to heed my uncle's warnings, but first he needed evidence to both prove *and explain* what he meant. When I moved to Asia, I found that evidence all around me—from family to employment to Christianity to local idol worship to news and current events. Every day, Asia proved that my uncle was right.

Not everyone had the dark ideology he had described. No one had it fully, many had it little-to-none, but everyone in Asia I met behaved as if somehow marked by it.

How could I ever prove whether my uncle's warnings were factual? These warnings are not taught in a living, mainline education stream. Any evidence would be old and dusty and, thus, might have only represented but a fringe in history.

But, when we look at the nation China is ripening into—and with it the very culture that Hong Kong, Taiwan, many American-born Chinese, and other Westernized Chinese are working desperately to escape—we see living evidence that those dark ideologies may very well had been widely held many generations ago. That would be the best explanation of why things today became as they are.

Then, we have some direct claims from Chinese today—that China believes they are the center of the universe, that they are shameless in saying so loudly and often. Old school *Nationalists* from Chiang Kai-Shek's party, just before their political humiliation in Taiwan's 2016 elections, boasted about their superiority as having "Han" blood (from the Han Dynasty.)

I have my own testimony, having sat with members of the Chinese government when they visited my college in 2001. At dinner, they insisted that only a global government could end war. I asked if they wanted to run that government themselves; they were speechless. I then asked if they wanted America to run that government; they were adamantly opposed. I asked if they saw the dilemma of who would run a global government; they had never thought about that before. Their intentions were all too clear.

There are indeed some loud claimants proving that this ancient, dark ideology lives today—but they could be minority, so we ought not trust those witnesses alone as general proof.

As I stated, the primary evidence that the Chinese-supremacist ideology was widely-accepted long ago is its wide impact, evident in today's Eastern Chinese cultures and the nation China is maturing into, towering right before our eyes, printing presses, and blogs.

So, from a rumored, near-legend past, reasonably explaining and confirmed by our world today, China's ambitions should be no surprise. That's all I argue.

I won't claim that Chinese *people* are "bad" or "disgusting" or anything of the kind. I only report that my uncle had words that explain things all too well, all too far in advance. Because of my uncle, news stories don't surprise me either. Lack of surprise has always been the thesis of these editorials.

China is a conquering nation with a long history of "peace through tyranny". That is the theme of most Chinese history movies. By contrast, American history movies are about "life through liberty". Both require blood of patriots and tyrants. In American stories the patriots are the good guys because they bring freedom. In Chinese stories, the tyrants are the good guys because they impose peace.

Hitler said the world needed Germany. Xi says the same about China. As the trends indicate, China won't stop its "reclaiming" at the nine-dash line it printed around the South Sea in its passport page artwork. China won't stop at flying its Chinese flag above every nation in the world. No. The ancient ideology that drives Chinese expansionism—whether confessedly stated outright or only in deed—evinces that it will never halt until all other ethnicities are eradicated and the only remaining race in the world is Han. As with Germany, those most unaware may be the Chinese themselves.

It is absolutely essential that we understand the ideologies that drive us. Usually, we don't. The more we understand our past and present days, the less our futures will surprise us.

What, then, drives the English-West? Post Rome and as English speakers, our own aims at global conquest take a different form than the Chinese, but some kind of drive is apparent in that we either colonize or we "intervene and help" in such a way that establishes a long-term presence around the world.

The Spanish were partially similar; consider Latin America. Likewise consider Portugal with Brazil and Macau or the Netherlands with their Formosan colony, today known as *Taiwan*.

Most of Europe might be able to argue that the Biblical *Great Commission*—to "go into all the world... and make disciples from every nation..."—drives Western "expansionism".

But, English culture has a deeper, older history of conquest that predates the Bible's influence.

The peoples of the British Isles were conquered and compounded into being, thereby creating the English hybrid language itself, the youngest and yet most widely shared common language in human history.

English culture does carry a *noble habitus* of Bible-based, hardy servanthood, but also an ironic value set of independence mingled with conquest—though demonstrable, the origin of this odd value set remains silent. But, Chinese imperialism has a loud explanation.

Today, Far East and Far West are colliding. This is world-shaping history and it is happening in our time. So, pay attention.

While I remember the words of my uncle, I also know the words of the Bible. In college, Bible was my major. I know that war must come because of how messed-up we are as humans. But, I also know that war is not the end.

Now, I don't believe in a strange, conquest-driven worldview of "making a new world from the ashes of the old". I don't favor Pyrrhic victories—which purport it be "good" for the victor to become King of the Rubble.

My belief that war is "necessary" is that our human foolishness makes it inevitable, not that war should be invited, welcomed, or celebrated.

Quite the opposite! If we offer patience and explanation to those around us, war might become a little less inevitable, even avoidable. But, to have this insight, we must not only inform our worldview with ancient legends of evil, but also consider the Bible that foretold the good ending, nearly 2,000 years ago.

Foreseeability is my theme, though I pretend no special insight. It doesn't take a spy to know China's ambitions, only a historian. It doesn't take a psychic to know that war is coming—and with it victory—, only a Bible student. By studying the past, we know what the future is like; and by including the Bible, we know that the far future is surely bright.

Editor Notes

These articles were originally published to online readers on the dates indicated. They were collected and first made available in this printed format in early 2019. In this printed edition, they have neither been reviewed nor edited. While these articles aim to be useful and informative, as editorials, they are not news, but *comment* on the news, and never at any time have they, nor any part of this book, made any claim as to fact.

The names of various editorial series follow musical terms, hence they are collectively called *Symphony*.

The *Voice* series is a "think piece" analysis of current events and is often irregular.

The theme of *Prelude* is that a military conflict was on its way. When shots were fired over the Myanmar-China border, I decided that the prelude in Asia was ended and that the conflict had begun.

The theme of *Cadence* is that a military conflict marches on, evident and already present, though it may still seem orderly.

The theme of *Encore* is that good days of renaissance, revival, renewal, reconciliation, and revitalization of a nation and its people are clearly on their way. It is not only the song itself, but also the applause leading to it.

The *2019 Preface* was written just before this first became available in print. I had been accused of being pro-China by siding against Taiwan in these articles. Both before and after, I was told that I was responsible for stirring distrust of China among Taiwanese—regardless of poll data showing that China needed no help courting distrust on its own, especially in its own backyard. Though strange, I thought about both accusations deeply and reconsidered whether I had a bias. Indeed, I had been overly charitable. I thus conceived and wrote the *2019 Preface* as consequence. The editorials printed here were not influenced or guided by this *2019 Preface*, rather the *preface* was developed from history unfolding, which, upon self-review, demanded that the *preface* was credible.

Articles by Date

2018

Encore of Revival: America, January 2

Terrorist talk didn't wait as the New Year arrived. Protests in Tehran have drawn two kinds of buzz: the first is that "keeping quiet" is the best way to respond, the second is that "economics" is the reason for the protests.

Taking the obvious first, people don't protest and riot merely over economics. This is a clear attempt by de facto pro- status quo pundits and media personalities to diminish the matter. Iranian people object to their government for the same reason everyone else does: it's a tyrant and terrorist-sponsoring regime. Reporting that the cause and headline-worthy DNA of the protests in Iran are merely about the "economy" is an insult to both the protesters and the protest victims.

The more complex buzz—claiming that the best response is to "keep quiet"—has several levels of "irony". Keeping quiet didn't work with getting Otto Warmbier back from North Korea—a friend of Iran —when Obama instructed the same tactic with Otto's family. So, "keeping quiet" has already proven to not work. Supporting protests discredits the protests and therefore gives more power to the current regime?—people in the press actually expect Americans to believe that? But, the largest of all contradictions coming from the Left relates to

Trump himself. If "keeping quiet" is the way to win, why doesn't the Left try "keeping quiet" about Trump, since they don't seem to be stopping him with their constant heckling?

Reactions and spin aside, the US is in "tyranny-crackdown" mode. Perhaps the Iranian people are taking to the streets because they finally believe that when America speaks something will actually happen. That has been the evidence of the last year, anyway.

Cadence of Conflict: Asia, January 2

China claims no part in the Hong Kong and Taiwan -related ships recently stopped by South Korean officials for illegally supplying oil to North Korea. China's claim might be believable, but during the holiday week, China blocked a UN attempted to blacklist those very vessels caught in the act. By blocking the block of the "smoking gun" ships, as it were, China has defined itself as an accomplice. It's a mere matter of fact and definition. There is no defense for China in regard to having some part to play with these two seized vessels.

Russia's role, however, seems more dominant and should be more disconcerting. But, where does the attention from the press turn to blame but China. The press loves to make China the global scapegoat, but China's responses don't help its own disposition any.

Beijing made it clear that military exercises all around Taiwanese airspace are the "new normal" and Taiwan will just have to get used to it. Taiwan is re-focusing strategy for asymmetric warfare— politically correct military language for "fighting a bigger enemy". Several Taiwanese companies are "rethinking" the presence of their factories in China after an entire zone was targeted for zone-wide shutdown. The catch to the zone shutdown story is that the entire zone is said to be targeted for a few blackout days because only some factories in the zone are polluting the environment too much. Factories that are within environmental regulations also have to shut down, argued to include Taiwanese-owned factories. Many factories in that zone are Taiwanese-owned. If China isn't sending a message that Taiwanese aren't welcome then Beijing could do a better job of not making it look that way.

Again, China's actions indicate more and more that China is hostile toward democracies in the East Pacific, namely South Korea and Taiwan. From the perspective of Americans reading Western headlines, it is more difficult every day to come to China's defense. That perspective among the masses is what the Pentagon is waiting for.

Encore of Revival: America, January 8

American news has a culture of rhetoric. People in that culture rehearse the "I'm really serious about this" tone, mannerisms, and gestures. They genuinely believe that "serious" delivery and well-distributed reports are the primary cause of public opinion. They think Trump was elected by mere propaganda and so they fight back with mere propaganda as if mere propaganda was the problem and its own solution. Now, it's more apparent than ever.

Since Trump announced, about 18 months ago, members of the "opinion class" have lived in a dream world that could not foretell the approaching train and cannot acknowledge the cause of the wreckage left when they wouldn't get off the tracks. And now, it seems that they think maintaining that dream will cast some magical, mind-control spell on the public.

Disassemble Wolff's comment, just as an example: "The economy is booming possibly because you'll have someone who's not capable of actually implementing any policies or regulation..." Since when did anyone in mainstream media believe that reducing government would help the economy? Then again, for people who think that rhetoric "trumps" results and that propaganda pulls rank over proof, such statements don't seem like a contradiction.

Take Jake Tapper's comment as he interrupted his guest, Stephen Miller: "I get it. There's one viewer that you care about right now and you're being obsequious… in order to please him." That video has been reposted and shared across the Internet, being viewed thousands of times just in the last day. No way was Miller speaking to only one audience member. Some may remember the incident for using big words many in the audience don't know, salacious and obsequious. But, few will notice that Tapper set a much more powerful precedent. By saying, "him," Jake Tapper is on well-viewed and -documented record as believing that it is not insulting to use the masculine pronoun when referring to an individual who could be of any gender. That also is a reversal from the mainstream mass media.

Then, low ratings in the NFL are being blamed on having too many games for fans to watch, even though the NBA has more games than people can watch and it's ratings are up through the roof. Since, as Wolff reports, the 25th Amendment is in discussion in so many places, perhaps it's time to speculate the hypothetical that the NFL protests could have been part of some conspiracy to raise NBA ratings. Merely discussing hypotheticals is all that matters for something to be worthy of reporting, right?

While the Left takes their turn objecting in their own way to the opposing agenda pushing through the White House, the Right are more interested in the mass media meltdown. At least that's how some people view it, but not everyone.

Cadence of Conflict: Asia, January 8

The talks between South and North Korea are not at all what they are cracked up to be. While the world would love to believe that this is some grand exercise in "can't we all just get along" diplomacy that always-only ever failed under Obama in any and every hemisphere, North-South talks are not what they seem. They are a distraction, a false pretense, an ostensible cover story, a smoke screen for something much, much deeper.

In all likelihood, the talks will include a very subtle Asian-style, excessively subtle (since it's among Koreans) offer. Even bachelor's degree students of business management study the science of talking to an employee in such a way that he doesn't figure out he's being fired until he gets home and takes his first bide of dinner. Leonardo explained the idea well in his movie Inception.

The meeting, capitalizing on participation in the Olympic games so strategically timed and placed, is more akin to the close of the series The Sopranos. A lieutenant of a rival family meets with the head of another family to plot the "offing" of his own boss in order to stop an ugly war that no one wanted, which started when that new boss came to power. The rival family "does in" their own boss at the gas station, the main character makes his hospitality rounds, and the story ends.

That's what this seems like. The Trump administration is allowing it, taking partial credit in a preemptive expectation of due accolades, also reminding the Asian world that communication is a good thing. Symphony said the same two days before Trump sent his January 4 Tweet to the same effect: without pressure from the US there would be no talks.

If Kim Jong Un eventually disappears in the months ahead, remember that it all came from this meeting, purportedly about the Olympics. There wouldn't be any moves in northern Korea without already having "certain assurances".

But, don't let that distract you. Taiwan is definitely playing its role in provocative and irksome "spitting matches" with China. As with the min-boss in The Godfather Part III, Taiwan wouldn't do that without "backing".

Encore of Revival: America, January 15

This was the week of rouses and houses. Trump called a bipartisan meeting from Congress at the White House and, to the surprise of many, much of the meeting showed on video. Everyone seemed to get along. Viewers could see real, actual video of leaders in real, normal conversation. It was somewhat unusual and not the least bit jarring.

Then began the rouse and purported fake news. The Wall Street Journal is accused of reporting that Trump claims a good relationship with Kim Jong Un rather than that he would have a good relationship with Kim Jong Un. This was one of the more obvious misreports. Another included Trump speaking vulgarly about unfortunate nations in his bipartisan meeting at the White House.

While there is no recording of his comments to members of Congress, there is a recording of what Trump said to the Wall Street Journal, which so far has refused to change the disputed quote.

Whether Trump actually spoke the dirty word as reported is left up to a whosaidhesaidit argument on Capital Hill. The big change: Republicans actually spoke in Trump's defense, that he didn't use such words. That should be notoriety enough, when someone receives support from his own enemies.

Then, there was the rouse in Hawaii with a false invasion alarm. Don't worry, Hawaii will think through what any Product Manager worth half of his salt would have drawn-up for a product roadmap well in advance. They will make it harder to press the "panic" button and equip their system with a "cancel" button to turn off the panic. Of course, it was all an accident and a big misunderstanding, nothing anyone needs to lose a job over.

In fact, the slew of rouses that trailed after the video of the president getting along with leaders in Washington was all a complete and coincidental "aligning of the planets", such a celestial event that does happen in nature, such as blue moons and Halley's Comet, except that the unusual string of rouses itself doesn't seem to be worth covering in the press—at least not elsewhere.

Cadence of Conflict: Asia, January 15

Jeffery Lewis at the Daily Beast has finally found a solution to the problem with North Korea: Kim Jong Un's port-a-potty. By bombing the dynastic successor's port-a-potty, the US would demonstrate both precision and presence. This would be the proverbial "arrow" from Robin Hood, conveniently shooting its way into the Sheriff's chamber.

Though the "papers" have not been "supplied" to top "brass" at press time, the premise has merit: showing that the US means business by "denying entry" for Kim to do his. While the "move" would surely cause an "emergency", their could be new security concerns about "individual privacy". The strategic proposal does not clarify whether or not to strike the "facility" while it is "occupied" by Kim "forces".

As for other port-a-potties in the region, China and Taiwan are deep in their own "potty" match. China is unilaterally opening new flight routs, reportedly in violation of agreements under the International Civil Aviation Organization. New flight routs are "required" to be coordinated first, but these were not. China simply "activated" them. The routs are very close to Taiwan airspace and Taiwan has made quite the buzz about it.

The US further complicated matters with a unanimously-passed bill from the House: the Taiwan Travel Act, which allows for high-level diplomatic visits between the US and Taiwan "under respectful conditions". The bill serves to support a shared "commitment to democracy". The House also passed HR 3320, which directs the Secretary of State to strategize for Taiwan to regain "observer status" at the World Health Assembly, which Taiwan failed to obtain in years past.

China made its own moves, particularly with doubts on the continued purchase of US Treasury bonds. That sent tremors through the markets in multiple directions.

Encore of Revival: America, January 22

The Russianewsgategate scandal is turning out even better for Republicans than was first anticipated. GOP members pretend to not be as excited and more surprised than they actually are —and they are also pretending to be quite angry, aghast, and indignant. In truth, Republicans finally found a way to go after some long-neglected corruption since they now have the socio-political wherewithal without starting a cycle of post-election political persecution.

Corruption is abundant. Even Amazon faces backlash after a suspicious settlement while contractors pass the buck. The biggest scandal of all: the lie that government shuts-down during a so-called "government shutdown". Some entitlements may be interrupted, but that's about all. A true shutdown of the government only exists in the most radical Conservatives' wildest dreams.

The tradition of panic over a rumored government shutdown dates back to the Clinton era when Bill vetoed the budget. Before then, no one dared touch a spending bill as it made way through the murky aisleways of Washington. It has since remained a threat politicians dangle over each other's heads in attempt to hold the American people captive to their petty partisan playbook. That myth, also, is being exposed.

Then there is immigration. Sanctuary cities are making themselves unpopular with flyover country. Administrative action to merely enforce existing law should soon be heard by the Supreme Court where Justice Kennedy will once again rule in favor of Justice Kennedy being the deciding swing vote who takes orders from no political party. Remember, Supreme Court justices always vote for the supremacy of the Supreme Court. The best guess is that his ruling will be half-and-half, mixed with a few doses of seemingly off-topic "surprise".

The American people are being played once again, from confronting corruption to budgets and bills. Washington could do much more, it's just waiting for the people to get all excited first. But, the Democrats may have overplayed their hand this time.

The premise behind Republican support for amnesty and programs like DACA was to gain votes by gaining new voters. The memo leaked from the Center for American Progress rallies the call that DACA is 'critical' to Democrats' 'future electoral success'. That basically suggests that Americans don't support Democrats—that Democrats don't serve their current voters.

Republicans spoke the same way during the Bush years; Jeb has piped in just to make sure the world knows that the Bush family still thinks that way. But, today's Republicans are starting to step away from all that rotgut and even push back on the "shutdown" threats.

Democrat politicians are now known to believe that a permanent class of voters dependent on government handouts is necessary to their future. DACA held a flickering hope of offering that. But, by shutting down the government to save DACA, the Democrats have alienated current voters dependent on those handouts. Their chances in 2018 look to be turning downward. It almost seems as if the Democratic party is self-destructing on purpose. And, that raises deeper questions.

Cadence of Conflict: Asia, January 22

Outcry against China over the Marriott crime of using the survey words "country" and "like" in reference to Tibet, Taiwan, and Hong Kong is over-rated. China has been shutting down propaganda channels and imprisoning people over such crimes for decades. But now, all of a sudden, China's routine becomes newsworthy? Something is amiss.

The press is stirring dissent against China in anticipation of a US-China conflict once the Korean situation is resolved. Without the Kim Dynasty, people won't be as panicked. Nothing will sell newspapers like a US-China war. Nothing helps a president get re-elected like a war supported by the public. To that end, everyone is playing their role perfectly.

The US-China conflict might be made possible merely because of Marriott's cleverly-worded survey. Marriott knew what they were getting into when they entered China's market. Marriott has lawyers and newspapers. Marriott should have known better. Management is lucky they are not being charged with attempting to appear as a public-stirring victim—like a Lusitania, Pearl Harbor, 9/11, Rosa Parks, or Trayvon Martin. The fact that China isn't pursuing Marriott for committing the crime on purpose begs the question: Does China understand the subtlety of Western mind games? Maybe they don't.

When the press remains free, authorities have to learn how to play more clever games, like Jackson, FDR, Reagan, Clinton, W. Bush, Obama, and Trump. When the press isn't free, authorities never develop those skills at playing games with the press. Those governments just print what they want without having to manipulate the press into thinking it was their own idea. If Marriott wanted to start a war, they got the press in both China and the US to print exactly what they wanted as masterfully as Donald Trump does. Does China recognize that or not?

It almost seems as if China wants to pay the West the courtesy of a warning shot across the bow: Exit now. That's the Western takeaway, anyhow. Everyone has their cultural DNA. Individual and societal culture can change, but slowly. When a person's individual culture easily and greatly offends a certain group of people, that person will avoid those people rather than change. If that person does change his culture to appease an easily-offended group, he will probably lose his friends. Either way, offense builds walls more than bridges. China is known for all three.

In the West, being easily offended is a sign of weakness, not strength. China's response will seem like an over-reaction in the US, thereby not only enraging Americans to support action against China, but emboldening them with the notion that the US would likely win—all on the grounds that Americans believe that easily-offended parties are weak. The strong don't care enough to be offended at all, right?

China's response, however, will embolden people within China. Any aggressive "power" assertion is seen by Chinese culture as a sign of strength and makes the masses gladly get in line. So, both the people of the US and China will be emboldened against each other—except of course for dissidents in both countries. US dissidents will hate the US, just as Chinese dissidents will hate China. That's what dissidents do.

The big lesson this week: Conflict is coming and everyone knows it. That's the only thing newsworthy. Reporting on the Chinese and Americans acting like Chinese and Americans is "news" so old, it's timing is mere propaganda.

Encore of Revival: America, January 29

The biggest problem with analyzing Trump's next move is speculation. Talk is talk, nothing more. America seems to be obsessed with talk far before action can confirm, acquit, deny, indite, prove, or disprove. We don't know what Trump will sign into law on Immigration until he signs it. But, he seems to be wise to America's priorities where talk and action are concerned. Once again, he plays the rhetoric-obsessed section of society like a harp. He makes an offer, he sends a Tweet, he proposes a bill, and everyone gets up and sings in concert.

Take the removal of Taiwan's "ROC" flag from the US government website as an expanded example. By not having any flag there, the flag can't be wrong. The original ROC flag has the symbol of the KMT-Nationalist party in the upper corner—the same party that lost both the presidency and the legislature for the first time in history during the last general election. Many have called for the flag to change. So, removing the flag from the website could mean that the US no longer supports the KMT-Nationalists. If Taiwan were to declare independence from the mainland, the US government wouldn't have the "wrong" flag on the website, nor if China were to attempt an invasion. While China may be thrilled and Taiwan may be angry, much more was involved by replacing the flag with pure white. Maybe "surrender" was the message, though it remains unclear to whom the word would be directed, even if that was the direction. What does remain clear is that the US government website is more important than anything else.

Once again, this time in the international sphere, the Trump administration won the war of words, this time without using any. What will happen, however, always remains yet to be seen until it happens.

Cadence of Conflict: Asia, January 29

It was a week of protests in both Hong Kong and South Korea. Neither side of any controversy rose above the fray. For the powers that be, it was PR gone bad. For the masses, it was spitting in the wind. When the governed don't want the ambitions of the controlling few, the solution is not Delphi method, but re-evaluation at the fundamental level. When the disgruntled masses reject the powers that be, peaceful boycott can make more lasting changes than any message sent by heated protest.

No one forced students to attend Baptist University in Hong Kong. If 90% of the student body objects to the mandatory Mandarin classes then 90% of the student body would do better to simply find another school. If the leadership at the university believes Mandarin classes can help students, then one would think the students would volunteer for them. A better way would be to make the classes both optional and tuition free for students and alumni of up to four years. If leadership is correct that the most widely-spoken language in the world, right in Hong Kong's back yard, would be useful for Hong Kongers—and classes with university credit were free for students and alumni—the university would see an influx of enrollment.

No one is forcing South Koreans to attend the Olympic Games. If South Koreans don't want the Kim Dynasty to participate in the games, they can save themselves the expense and either save the time of going or replace that time with a public stand-in, carrying educational signs during the Olympics, whether on-sight or off. If the democratic South Korean government wants to promote a unified stance with North Korean athletes, they can use the abundance of Internet technology to poll the public on what would make the people happy to that end. Since South Korea's new president is so popular, he should not have lacked feedback when asking his many supporters what they want to do.

Taiwan made it's own—and likely most aggressive—move. By entering the world of AI development, Taiwan is entering the ring with other big players, such as China. Few will see it as the bold move that it is. The miracle of Taiwan's AI venture was that the move did not insight protests.

The only positive communication seemed to be between China and Japan. They are communicating about communicating. That's always a good thing.

Encore of Revival: America, February 5

Machines are trying to take over. They aren't winning. And, they aren't mechanical machines made of steel and iron alloys—or in GM's case also aluminum. These are machines of "big money". Some of them are political, some of them are from the entertainment industry, others are in the business world.

Ultimately, the machines run round and round by creating problems, then solving them.

Nestle has been taking water from Springhill in Osceola County, Michigan for nearly two decades. Locals have battled with the water-relocating giant almost as long; the State often comes to Nestle's defense. We'll see how much longer that lasts. The current battle seems to include no third-party scientific research, only claims by locals that water levels are lowering vs claims by Nestle that Nestle isn't hurting anything and that local water costs would rise without Nestle—which is at the same time accused of causing the water shortage in the first place. It's almost a self-inditing argument in Nestle's defense. Now, Nestle wants to take more water.

Then, there's Uma. Perhaps "Kill Bill" should have been renamed to include something about a guy named "Harvey", at least if the title reflected the emotions of "what the movie advertisements called a 'roaring rampage of revenge'" from what happened on set and behind the scenes. To this point, Symphony has not focused on Weinstein stories because, so far, they didn't seem to include news. Uma's story in the New York Times, however, introduces the video of her injury during a stunt she was intimidated into doing. After 15 years, she finally got her hands on the video. Uma just might mark the beginning of Vol. 2 in brining down scandal-filled Hollywood.

Then, there's the machine that's after Trump. According to the president, it's a disgrace, people should be ashamed, and Congress will do what Congress will do, which is fine. Bias against Trump is "yuge". In one man-on-the-street video by Campus Reform, people react negatively to State of the Union comments—until they realize they were made by Obama. Democrats and the mainstream media can't halt the assault against Trump as long as that widespread bias against Trump exists in such a large segment of the voting population. But, that bias is driving the anti-Trump machine to uncover more and more dirt—not on Trump, but dirt—on Democrats.

While Nestle seems to solve problems it causes, the Left caused the problems it's solving. As for Hollywood, the movies describe it best.

Cadence of Conflict: Asia, February 5

Writing about China is difficult. On one side there is the Western push toward the false narrative that "all things China are bad", then on the other side pulls gravity from an invisible black hole gobbling up the truth. China is a yeah-boo, more yeah and more boo than most other countries. Anyone expecting a narrative—West or East—while reading the truth about China might instinctively think that the truth supports "the other side".

But, Symphony doesn't take that stance. China is just China. It makes wise moves, it makes foolish moves, just like every other nation on Earth.

This week was a week of economics. China is cracking down on cryptocurrency—just as it cracks down on anything it can't control with externally-applied force. The cryptocurrency market in China is fleeing from the crackdown. Yet, China is reaching out to Europe and Britain.

While the economy in Europe is big on China's list, so is the Vatican. Now, the Vatican wants an unholy marriage with China similar to the one with Medieval Europe: Beijing and the Vatican choose Chinese bishops and the underground Church gets pulled out from underground. In other words, both Western and Eastern powers crush the little guy.

This will actually cause the underground Church in China to grow even more.

Just how control is driving away cryptocurrency, so will Sino-Vatico control drive the underground farther underground. Like jell-o in the hand, tightening the grip makes them slip through the fingers. A better solution would have been, more or less, status quo: Let China keep doing whatever they want and let the Vatican excommunicate whomever they want. But, the Vatican knows that would be the better solution. Does China know that the Vatican knows?

Any kind of agreement between the Vatican and China is pointless since China doesn't plan to ever compromise anyway, especially on the Vatican's human rights agenda as well as Taiwan. In the end, Catholics worldwide will hate China more. China should avoid all talks with the Vatican because any Westerner can foresee that it will only reap ill will in the West. Perhaps that is the Vatican's deeper agenda in "making a deal with the dragon", as it were. If China is the tiger then the Vatican is the monkey; the tiger has been warned.

China making infrastructure and economic inroads to Europe, is a good thing, but not on most levels people consider. Firstly, it is an indication that China feels a squeeze from the US and is looking for new trading partners. Secondly, it will cause the Westernization of China more quickly. Europe and Britain don't like dishonesty. Many of the dishonest practices Chinese businessmen are notorious for—which the Communists are cracking down on for the record—won't be tolerated. In terms of "ethics", China will have to Westernize in order to do business with the West. Perhaps that is why Beijing is pushing it—to help with the crackdown.

The second matter is more militarily strategic. To governments, all infrastructure is military infrastructure. If China has a roadway into Europe, that is a roadway that can be used by an army—in either direction. So, finances between China and Europe carry two approaching stigmas: 1. China's power is morphing into economics and 2. China is laying-in wartime infrastructure.

Changing to an economic power will weaken China's ability to use military force. Taiwan is making economic power moves of its own by positioning itself to become an AI development hub for the world—which China's customers could likely be dependent on if they aren't already. No one wants to drop bombs on customers, yet China is busily making both.

These economic relations will "tame the dragon", as it were, which may not be what China wants. Secondly, Europe is inviting China to become a stronger military power in their own back yard. China is no traitor, but nor are the Chinese loyal to anyone but the Chinese. Russia should try to halt China's relations with Europe for Russia's own good. Believe it or not, China may hold Russia in check before this is all over. Making inroads for

China might be Europe's salvation in decades to
come.

Encore of Revival: America, February 12

The budget deal in Congress declares two myths, one from time travel budgeting, the other from silence. When the "experts" project a deficit based on the current spending plan, 1. none of the money has been spent yet and 2. none of the spending tax money has come in yet. They aren't only counting chickens before they hatch, they already have them buttered on the Christmas dinner table.

The spending projection assumes the previous year's tax income. If tax rates drop, so does the projected income drop, proportionately. There is some "trickle down" account for the assumption that consumers may spend more and employers hire more since they have the funds not taxed, but they don't consider synergy. They don't use AI simulations to project the slew of companies who haven't announced—but will anyway do—investment within the market. New companies will be capable of coming into being which weren't able to without the new financial ecosystem. Those aren't accounted for because they can't be predicted. The forecast we have is based not on synergistic outcomes—AKA reality—but on comparing last years results against this year's new methods—AKA time travel.

The second myth comes from silence, namely renegotiating trade agreements. Adjustments making the US market part of a two-way street will also bring new revenue sources—rather than a one-way street that screws the US economy into the ground. These are part of separate agreements already promised, already underway, but largely unfinished and unreported. Budget forecast about those factors are simply silent.

The budget forecast isn't any accurate prediction of the future, but a kind of comparison for number geeks in black-tie offices. What actually happens is never known until it happens.

Cadence of Conflict: Asia, February 12

There are those who know Asia and those who don't. There are those who know political gaming and those who don't. Last week, Symphony said that China wouldn't compromise in a "Sino-Vatico" deal. This week, a retired bishop in Hong Kong said basically the same thing: That if the pope vetoes Beijing too often, Beijing will tell the world the pope is unreasonable.

The pope is no fool. The Vatican knows to listen to a Hong Kong bishop concerning China. The deal is hotly debated in the Church and by no means unanimously supported as motherhood or apple pie. If the Vatican goes through with this controversial deal with China, then it indicates that the Vatican is counting on a popularity war against China, in which China loses respect, both among Catholics in China and everyone in every economy everywhere else in the world, except of course among Russians who always like a good fight.

If war breaks out between the West and China, and if China loses to a fierce West, China ought hold the Vatican partially responsible for playing the complex popularity mind game which is this deal. This agreement was always a cloaked plan to harm

China. It seems that the retired bishop in Hong Kong hasn't figured that out.

The Vatican would have us believe that they haven't figured out China when they actually have things figured out all to well. That's what makes the Vatican arguably the greatest danger to China. No wonder China is so concerned, but still not concerned enough.

Equally concerning, Taiwan is seriously talking about moving their Legislative Yuan and their Executive Yuan offices with it. The new location would be Taichung, the center of Taiwan. That would put the central government seat in two locations and the frequent target of democratic demonstrations between the ideologically conflicted north and south. While this is purported to help connect the central government more closely to local governments—and to provide large, open plazas so that demonstrations don't interrupt local commerce—and to provide for an "earthquake" not disrupting the entire central government, that word "earthquake" carries symbolic meaning without mention. A change of cartography will also date any invasion rehearsals.

More than implicating an airborne "earthquake" from, say, China, promoting democracy demonstrations along with a united island of 23 million are the greater, yet more subtle, messages that may insult some offices on the other side of that Taiwan strait. Few in the West will understand how Taiwan's central government creating a "second seat" could spark the war that the Vatican is already piping the popularity to fuel.

Just as much, there are those who do and do not understand North Korea. Every time the West is shown media coverage of North Korea, journalistic commentary doesn't know what to say. *Look at them, they all clap in unison. Doesn't it look strange? They can't be happy; after all they never stop smiling. It's all fake. And, look at all of the crying at the Kim Jong Il funeral. That's either fake or it's radical support.*

The press, wholly unqualified to explain events in Far East Asia, can't help but flaunt their own ignorance.

North Koreans are part of a tightly-controlled, cult-like, nannied-and-mommied play script. They are neither happy nor sad. They are caught in a culture of mass group think. They cry at a Kim funeral because that's what you do, much like taking your shoes off at the door. They cheer in choreographed unison at a sports arena because that's what you do at sports arenas and, more importantly, all cheering is choreographed anyway, right?

They aren't cheering from any obligation. They're like a bunch of Sunday Morning micro-church minions parroting their microcosm lingo because that's the only thing they have ever learned to do. A similar comparison would be to tone-lexical native language speakers—such as Cantonese and Mandarin—trying to use the free-form tone flow of

Romance sentences, or asking someone who only
reads sheet music to improvise for the first time
ever. Singing spontaneously from the heart just
isn't something they have ever known. And, all the
Western press can do is gawk, but not understand.

It just shows how far we still have to go to get to
know each other.

Encore of Revival: America, February 19

No one likes to read about school shootings. I was in high school when a student shot himself in the head, right in the hallway, Vinnie Garofalo, February 1998. I remember when a college classmate told our student body the reports from his former classmates at Columbine. "They're dead," she told him. "They're all dead." Now, the Editor needs to write about it and Americans need to read about it, yet again.

The Florida shooting is complicated, it always is. This one has a story behind the shooter that seems more personal than other times. No one claims his story is any alibi. Many heroes were made, both victim and living. One libriarian, Diana Haneski, was inspired by her friend's heroism from Sandy Hook and protected 55 students by locking them in a media room. An assistant coach, Aaron Feis, protected three girls by shielding them with his own body, he did not survive.

Tragedy strikes. We reflect and ask why. Then we second guess ourselves and wish that we would have loved each other more and sooner. We go home. We cry ourselves to sleep. Then we wake up the next day and prepare to march for action. So, let's talk action.

Emma Gonzales is right, in a sense even the minds of gun owners. To the gun owners, the NRA has been largely useless. They aren't effective at protecting gun owner rights, only at rallying people up. At Columbine and with Michael Moore, the NRA's reaction was generally useless. Rather than helping the nation navigate through the challenges, they just acted insensitive. The NRA's Twitter account hasn't posted since Valentine's Day, when the Florida shooting happened, not even sympathy to the families. This seems to have been a "silencer" for the NRA. Politicians who receive money from that over-spiced "nothing burger" organization should be ashamed.

As for action, since we act like we're ready for a candid conversation, let's take off the gloves. Before you decide to click "next", finish the next two paragraphs.

Why are we in deadlock about guns? As strong—and correct—of an argument as Emma Gonzales makes, there is another strong point that must be included in our united path forward. It's the "elephant" in the living room, the reason we can't finish the debate, which no one wants to so much as even mention. The dirty, politically incorrect, and inconclusive—mind you—little secret about why guns remain widely available on the market has three big beans: Russia, China, and ISIS. The wide-availability of guns in America is the only reason those countries—ISIS is a country—have not already invaded and killed millions of Americans—just as their governments have killed millions of their own people who aren't allowed to possess guns. That's our excuse that keeps us in deadlock over the gun debate—a deadlock that killed 17 people last Valentine's Day.

The problem is not the Second Amendment itself, but that we only enforce half of it. We need the rest of the Second Amendment—the Militia army of civilians—a high school class with accommodation for handicapped and learning disabled, different standards for different gender, and it would be a requirement for every student in order to graduate and in order to vote in elections. The high school Militia course would teach self-discipline, readiness, hand-to-gun combat, safety in every situation, gun handling and discharge, emergency response, teamwork, and, like all military training, self-respect and self-sacrifice for others. If Nikolas Cruz had been required to graduate high school before he could buy a gun, he wouldn't have been able to. If he had been required to get the mentoring a high school Militia class would have provided, he wouldn't have wanted to.

That idea has been presented before by many people before. But, we don't hear about it from the NRA. We didn't want to have such a candid discussion about applying the whole of the Constitution—which would keep us safe from enemies, both foreign and domestic, if we would simply obey it to the full. We were too distracted with other news. So, since those other news items that we bicker about were worth the lives of 17 students, let's take a review of the news items atop headlines in the days before the Valentine's Day Massacre...

The Obama portraits, while acceptable, are intended to draw attention. The Smithsonian has more expressive art of Ford and HW Bush, more radical than the Michelle interpretation. Contrary to folk wisdom, the woman in the painting does resemble Michelle in those rare moments when she drops that goofy, fake smile for her natural "serious" face. It's not that strange, as strange as it seems. But, the hue of the leaves in Obama's piece and the street-art worthy style of Michelle evince an intent to use the presidential portraits as an opportunity to make some kind of statement. Whether that is right or wrong is up for debate, but they are trying to make a statement.

As for the leaves, to claim that they are marijuana is to claim either that the artist is botanically inept or that oneself is. The leaf in the picture more resembles the Ohio State "buckeye leaf", which has been confused by the botanically inept in the past.

Michael Flynn was pursued by Obama's leftover administration as retribution for endorsing Trump. It is said one should never hire friends. Hiring Flynn was a mistake, not because Flynn wasn't up to the job of fighting in the wolf den—which he apparently wasn't—but because it promoted him from being a target to being an easy target. In the end, however, Michael Flynn will learn just as Sarah Palin did, after being tossed to the wolves. And, the hostile takeover of Flynn's life will be an alarm in itself to call out the folks to find out just what in the world was going on in the Obama administration that allowed this to happen. Flynn will come back to haunt the Democrats and bureaucrats.

George Soros has been dumping money into local DA elections that would normally elect Republicans. His candidates have been winning. Democrats and their voters who don't stand against Soros will lose all credibility when next time they complain about the Koch brothers. While many Republican voters will be alarmed—and probably roused to a wrath those DAs will not want to face—the more interesting effect will be their tendency to self-destruct. People artificially propped into power rarely last, especially when they come from different stock.

...But, there's nothing like a school shooting to put our priorities about the news in perspective.

Cadence of Conflict: Asia, February 19

Conveniently, Axios breaks a story from Trump's November visit to China. There was a scuffle and a tackle over the "nuclear football"—AKA the nuke code bag. At first, it seems like relations are breaking down between the US and China. At second glance, the timing of the report is outright suspicious. Stepping back and giving it a third thought, the scuffle almost seems prophetic and poetic about the American-Chinese situation. The Chinese didn't touch the "nuclear football", though there was an ignored or unreceived memo. The US entourage kept moving. The Chinese official in charge kindly apologized. And, it was all over in an instant and without incident. That seems to have a figurative application on a literary level.

China is expanding in science and other areas. Underwater drones capable of making military maps were told to be for science only. Mischief Reef's new missile-defense equipped naval-air bases were only for a fishermen's shelter. And, the first aircraft carrier, the Liaoning, was purchased from Russia to be nothing more than a floating museum. Those kinds of stories get drummed up by the West as reasons not to trust China.

The Philippines have effectively made peace with China on some level. China is capable of preserving peace if it wants to. But, the Western press often points to grandiose statements that rub Westerners the wrong way. President Xi referred to the belt road project as the "project of the century" and that it will "add splendor to human civilization". The West cares about taxpayer efficiency, freedom to have children, and welcome open dissent against their own government. Westerners value humility from leadership. The Chinese grandiose remarks from Xi Jinping command respect in China, but are off-putting to Westerners. Rather than seeking to reconcile the differences in rhetorical preference, press reports exploit the shock value and sell-out peaceful understanding for caustic sensationalism. The divide grows. Whether China should tone down its language is a Chinese-internal decision. So is the opinion and response by the West also a purely internal decision.

So, at the same time Axios reports a non-incident story of a conflict that didn't happen over a "football" last November. It is framed as a sign of shaky US-China relations. Others are reporting on the US, Japan, Australia, and India collaborating competition against China's infrastructure. There is also news of Trump buckling down on trade with China. Then, Quartz publishes a review of China's great threat as a rising military power, a collection of old news.

Truth or lie, propagandized or unbiased, the timing is a tell-all. The Western press is preparing the public for war.

Encore of Revival: America, February 26

If we look at help and mutual interests, it would seem that the NRA is a covert Leftist organization and that anti-gun groups sponsor gun shows.

The best reasons and the best laws for gun owners are also the best-kept secrets, at least in NRA memes and Tweets. Gun owners often say that "gun control" means "hitting your target", but where are the NRA bumper stickers calling for target practice, for high school students to take the Constitutionally required "Militia" course? It doesn't have to be in high school, but high school makes the most sense since both Militia and high school education are performed by the State. By only rallying for guns, guns, yeah, yeah, the NRA seems to be making its own strawman defense for guns—giving the wrong reason for a half-right conclusion. It invites effective opposition.

Gun shows have a similar irony. Every time anti-gun laws are even discussed, gun sales go up. Florida just saw record attendance at a recent gun show.

Either the two groups are in cahoots or they don't really think about the effects of their actions.

Taiwanese young men are required to attend a weekly class in high school as part of mandatory basic military training. After they have been out of school for a certain period of time, they are summoned by their government to report for four weeks of on-sight basic training. Their society does not have any guns in circulation, except the police, of course, and what unproven political-mafia machines might allow into the hands of "enforcers", but that's a different story. Taiwan's society is light years safer than American.

The two cultures are very different. The United States has wide, open country where police response time is slower than the second-most densely populated country in the world. But, if basic military training can keep a gun-free society safe, imagine what already Constitutionally-required "Militia" training would do for the USA.

Cadence of Conflict: Asia, February 26

It's hitting the fan. China is homing-up and the US is "posseing" up. CFIUS is expanding its scope and China just required Apple to send its iCloud encryption keys to servers on the mainland. Both moves are more about caution than provocation. The US is stepping up patrols to enforce the trade block on North Korea. China just started the process of amending its Constitution to remove terms limits on its President.

The change to China's Constitution is often mis-portrayed. It affects both the President and Vice President. It does not install a President for life, but simply allows it. More importantly, the Constitution is being updated to include the "Xi Thought", mainly that all ethic groups of China are equal and that helping the entire world is part of China's responsibility.

Many in the West will jump to presume Xi is making a grab for power. While it does increase his power, the more accurate interpretation is that Xi's plans go for the long term, specifically after Trump's term. Without this change, Xi would leave office by 2023. China is thinking in terms of long-term, global strategy. That's hardly a "grab", but more of a "waltz".

This is a significant change. Both the US and China clearly mean business. With a shift toward the long-term, and with China publishing its view that the whole world is part of its responsibility, we are in a different political atmosphere than in years past.

Encore of Revival: America, March 5

Everything happening in Washington news right now means absolutely nothing.

Gun legislation means nothing—bills will get passed, but the public hasn't heard about those bills yet. There just hasn't been enough time to draft and debate them.

Security clearances get adjusted all the time. Politicians meet and talk all the time—a president who has actual negotiation experience, however, might seem a little surprising to people who don't understand Trump. But, none of it is news and none of it will go anywhere. It's all one big, giant distraction for what is actually developing, which we should see in the coming weeks and months.

The only thing that happened of significance was the US Senate's unanimous passage of the "Taiwan Travel Act", which would basically allow Trump to visit Taiwan and vice versa, as well as many other officials, and, of course, irritate the Chinese. Unanimous passage of a Senate bill? Why didn't that make headlines from a press obsessed with "bipartisan cooperation"?

It didn't make headlines because everything happening, this week anyway, is just a distraction

from what's really going on, whatever "else" that
may be, in addition to Asia.

Cadence of Conflict: Asia, March 5

China's changes include finances as well as politics. As the US unrelentingly inches toward absolute denuclearization of North Korea—one way or another—China delays solidarity at the UN. China has no lack of mixed messages in other areas, such as Taiwan.

Stepping up military drills near Taiwan while becoming more economically friendly to Taiwanese isn't exactly something that causes democratic voters to fall in love with a nation without elected official term limits. Some Taiwanese will take advantage of the economic favoritism, but those will probably be the kind of companies run by bosses who have a moderately high turnover rate coupled with complaints about overbearing, old school Asian leadership style. When China suddenly changes colors again, they could lose their companies, all depending on what Chinese "national security interest" needs arise with the sun. That will become an unanticipated economic edge to "isolationist" companies that remain in Taiwan and prefer a "flattened-out" administrative structure. Notwithstanding, experts claim it could all backfire.

Then there is Korea and Vietnam. China won't need to worry about US intervention stealing its customers in North Korea much longer since that customer will soon cease to exist. Calling off a potential meeting between Pyongyang and Washington officials at the Winter Games involved Kim Jong Un's sister being present. It indicates paranoia; Un is evidently concerned about a coup. He should be. Many of his officials had just jumped decades forward in time travel, also called "crossing the border", when they saw the life, joy, happiness, technology, and pleasures of the modern world. Top North Korean brass will pine to return and Un's sister knew they would. Calling off the meeting only alerted the world to Pyongyang feeling threatened.

So much said in a denial. US Congress unanimously passes the "Taiwan Travel Act", essentially allowing every diplomat even up to Trump and Tsai to meet face-to-face, in public, in celebratory AKA "respectful" conditions. But, the US media—always asking for bipartisanship— doesn't care to report the passage of the unanimous bill. That means that the bill may actually accomplish something, and that is why China is furious, depending on the occasion of course.

The US sending 5,000 troops to stop in Vietnam for the first time in 40 years should be more disconcerting to China that the passage of any bill or the blockage of any trade ships with North Korea. Of course, China says that they have no interest disturbing the international status quo and they respect other countries, albiet the "Xi

Thought" includes, more importantly than removal of term limits, that the entire world is China's responsibility.

While the West would paint China as a villain, nothing could be farther from the truth. After all, a police officer didn't even need permission to catch a girl falling from the forth floor. Her grandmother had locked herself outside of her own apartment and the key smith scared the girl into climbing out the window. The police officer caught the girl, both were hospitalized. And, of course, ruling party officials from China made sure to visit and congratulate the officer for such quick thinking.

Then, we have Google and Apple courting more favor with China. Maps and Translate are back, with a China-controlled remix, of course. National security is vital. But, therein lies a cloaked warning. China is already under attack by the West. Soon-to-be non-Communist and united Korea, US-Friendly Vietnam, soldiers waiting to flex their muscles in India, diplomatic visits to Taiwan, not to mention the ever pro-US Japan— China is surrounded.

This is dangerous. All that needs to happen is for China to send out its military like King John's Crusade, then Apple and Google will have no opposition re-educating China's population, without soldiers to protect what's happening at home. It would be best for China to refortify and give Apple and Google the boot, but who is the West to give China any suggestion. The West has

money and power, so they clearly don't
understand.

We live in historic times.

Encore of Revival: America, March 12

Scott Walker is self-destructing and may not win a third term. It began in his bid for the presidency when his campaign imploded. Initially, he over-reached. He was too much good for Wisconsin too fast and he wasn't prepared to take on the wolves. Given the sudden spotlight, he aimed for the presidency. Now, he's talking like George HW Bush when he reneged on his "read my lips, no new taxes" speech, then said he needed to raise taxes to get along with Democrats toward the end of his first—and hence final—term. If Walker doesn't lose, then there either aren't any good Republican or Democratic candidates in Wisconsin or history has decided to stop delivering justice upon those who don't learn from it.

SpaceX is proving the benefits of both public funding and privatization. Surely both Liberals and Conservatives will want the claim. The US government paved the way for space exploration, but Elon Musk made the stage-one booster return to the landing pad. The world has not seen a breakthrough of this magnitude since Lincoln regulated the first transcontinental railroad through the government while it was built by competing private companies.

Californian idealists, whether right or wrong, are distracted. If they truly believe in their ideals to stand against the Federal government, they will need to stop ballyhooing sanctuary city talking points and repeal their anti-gun laws. Right now, California's best friend is not social media, but the Second Amendment, specifically the part about a State-regulated militia. Many claim that the National Guard is the militia, but that idea has not been fully tested and vetted and it also has many categorical questions. Calling the national guard to stand against the US military might not work, though it's a good guess the idea has been tossed around at least one conference room in the bowls of California's state capitol. We'll just have to wait and see.

Cadence of Conflict: Asia, March 12

As talks between Kim and Trump march forward, China is resigned to the new situation at its eastern border and is focusing on other areas, specifically trade. In truth, China's main trade opponent is not the US, but Vietnam.

Vietnam's main edge in trade will be that it is less expensive. Vietnam is, in many ways, less developed, yet more free to be expressive. Hanoi doesn't sanction the same censorship as Beijing does. Many hard-working Vietnamese are hungry, even desperate for income. A hard-working, uncensored, hungry, less-expensive people will be difficult for China to compete with on many fronts. This is entirely beside any point about political tension between China and Vietnam.

The meeting between Kim and Trump is less-than-satisfactorily explained. Suddenly they want to talk? Some "teamwork" consultant trying to sell a book will likely attribute it all to diplomacy, along with the preemptive speculation that Kim would give up the nukes because he got them. More is going on behind the scenes and if the true story is ever told it may not be told for ten or twenty years.

As for the Western spin about China's constitutional changes, it is all about the party, not about Xi. The humble pig farm worker, Xi Jinping, did not rise to power by publicly trying to serve himself. He has followed Robert Greene's 48 Laws of Power to a tee and will continue to do so—that means putting the party first in his public agenda.

Encore of Revival: America, March 19

General Michael Flynn has earned a purple heart. The corruption against him indicated by text messages is scandalous. The public will rally to his defense more and more.

Trump allows Mueller to continue, indicating strength not weakness. Trump is letting Mueller proverbially "hang himself", or to be "Biblical", build his own Haman scaffold. Lashing out at Mueller on Twitter comes from Trump's "social nose" telling him to wait for public support so that when—not if—Trump fies Mueller, the public demands more investigations of the draining swamp, which still will not satisfy the public outcry against corruption.

By not yet taking so much action as demanded, Trump opponents will see him as moderate and his support could even increase in the 2020 election— already likely to increase since the normal mid-term losses long predicted by Symphony will only rouse Trumpists to get out the vote even more.

The Facebook scandal involving the said-to-be-dubious research group Cambridge Analytica neither indites Democrats nor Republicans since the group is likened to "mercenaries" who will work for anyone's pay. It does raise questions about Facebook's inside baseball, though at most

Facebook's involvement seems to have been not caring enough or not having policies prepared to handle what Cambridge Analytica was doing, but we'll have to wait and see. Nonetheless, Facebook will end up being more regulated by Congress, something quite easily done through FTC regulations—Facebook is a company with publicly traded stock. We could see legislation imposing a kind of "fairness and privacy doctrine" on public social media companies. Facebook is becoming a de facto utility, a status clearly proven by how important it was to Cambridge Analytica.

The STOP, School Violence Act of 2018 sponsored by Orrin Hatch has due bipartisan support. It also contains provisions for training, something suggested by Symphony just after the Florida Valentine's Day Massacre. Democrats naturally want more, but are supportive.

Cadence of Conflict:
Asia, March 19

Unlike much of the Western press, Pacific Daily Times does not side with governments, political parties, or socio-economic ideologies. The Times only sides with history, that by learning from history much of the future is foreseeable. Foreseeability, based on history, is the only bias at Pacific Daily Times.

Foreseeability is not preference, hopes, or will—good or ill—toward what will happen, only that the future can, to the extent history repeats, be reasonably anticipated. Too many news outlets seem incapable of understanding that predicting outcomes, within reason, is entirely different from hoping for outcomes. Predicting and hoping are nothing alike. Pacific Daily Times is apathetic and indifferent—uncaring and cold-hearted—for how the future unfolds, except that current events only surprise neglectful history students.

Right now, foreseeability in Asia—not what is hoped-for in Asia—points to the waring parties of China. The KMT-Nationalist party and the Chinese Communist Party seem to have a symbiotic relationship. Their fates seem tied like the villain and hero of some comic series, if the hero kills the villain then both die and vice versa. The KMT-Nationalist party imploded on its home field in

Taiwan. It was so distracted with "reunification" with China that it neglected the priorities that kept its power. As a result, Taiwan is run by the de facto pro-independence Democratic People's Party. The KMT failed to help its CCP friends across the Taiwan Strait because it was overly obsessed with that friendship.

Now, it seems that the CCP is headed in the same direction. Without fear or favor, only calculating predictability based on the past, it seems we could be looking at the beginning of the end of the CCP. Every party that rises too high tumbles, history has executed this with zero exception and will never accept rivals. History demands that history always be the only victor by making all others history.

Since the founding of the current Chinese government in 1912, which the "Chinese year" commemorates, China has confronted its own shame, which it still confronts to this day. The founder, Sun Yat-sen, was a Christian whose Christianity compelled him to the three pillars of Chinese society: nationalism, democracy, and justice for the people. Though the largest nation, China has never been the most powerful nation. Centuries of "leader power distance" touted oppression as "peace-making" virtue. Some say it worked for China, others say it failed for China. Actually, it was the only thing that happened in China, so there is no basis of contrast to prove definably whether that Chinese power distance ethic succeeded or failed except that it brought

China to 1911 where Sun defeated it. While the power distance left in the form of a government "empire", it has neither left the ideology nor the mode of operation in Chinese culture, as repeating history proves once again this month.

Xi Jinping's thinking remains uncertain. What motivates him? We really don't know beyond the evidence that his thinking reflects Mao and traditional pre- Sun Yat-sen power distance. He doesn't want shame for his country and he believes that reclaiming all land from every "old turf war" dispute will make the world think China as worthy of being respected. The rest of the world will decide its own opinion, but Chinese history has its own opinion about Xi.

Xi, as many in China, have loudly declared that they neither import nor export their politics. But, Communism is itself form Europe. Chinese people study English and gladly import Western technology and money while exporting goods to the West. But, most importantly of all, Sun Tzu's Art of War Ch. 8, ss. 12's "five dangerous faults" include: 3. a hasty temper provoked by insult and 4. a delicacy of honor sensitive to shame. Whenever Taiwan hints at "independence" or the US sails through UN-international waters which member China disputes, an explosion of rage and demands plume from Chinese press offices. Then we have the insatiable need for respect, the motive behind China's desire for reunification with many lands, only one of those being Taiwan. Sun Tzu warned against these ideologies nearly a thousand years ago.

China has often misunderstood Christianity. Just as with Confucianism, there is the essential belief and then the government exploitation of it. Most "missionaries" are advancing a government-corporate hybrid, usually known as a "denomination" with an administrative and monetary structure. Jesus did not teach this. Chinese often view Christianity as a religion between God and Man while Confucianism teaches relationship between one Man and another. But, Jesus taught that God and Man is the archetypal relationship guiding the equally important practical application of the relationship between one Man and another. The emphasis on the relationship between God and Man to the exclusion of peer relationships came from European imperial governments misinterpreting the Bible and exploiting people's ignorance of Jesus's true teaching.

The great mystery of how the West gained such power and success without the Confucian-preferred version of an "ordered society" remains in the real Jesus. The founders of America, the Pilgrims, studied the Bible to love God as individuals—free from European government misinterpretation and control of the Bible—so they would love each other. All of this Bible study was done as individuals who loved God and had zero government control.

The mess in the West today, interfering with China along with the rest of the world, is an attempt from old oligarchs trying to reassert their power over a free, Bible-reading people. Xi Jinping is fighting against that same old oligarchy as the American people are. Corptocratic chronyism of the West is a problem everywhere. Xi Jinping is trying his best, with good will, to overcome it. But, he owes more to Sun Tzu's Chinese wisdom and he is trying to overcome ancient evils of the West without first seeking to understand what virtues of the real Bible made the West so strong in the first place. As for whether and how it works out, history will have the last word as it always does.

Encore of Revival: America, March 26

David Hogg is right, but the Hollywood Left is trying to exploit him. Baby Boomers have failed to manage their Democracy, along with their kids, and however that generational chain works its way into the students currently in school. Clear backpacks are, best put, "stupid". Showing girls' tampons in the hallway and letting all students spy in each other's bags doesn't stop a gunman from hurting people. But, that comes from common sense, not the 1st Amendment.

The 2nd Amendment is David Hogg's best friend. The best way to restrict guns in America is to deny them to everyone who has not completed the Constitutional mandate for all-citizen militia training. Hogg doesn't care about scrapping it nor about Left or Right politics, though the Left capitalizes on him and his friends. That, too, could backfire.

In all this, David Hogg and his classmates are doing the country a great and wonderful favor: They are getting involved in politics as they should be. One does not need to be a Constitutional expert, we just need to be involved, even with much yet to learn. Bravo, David! Had high school students been so concerned 20 years ago we would not have the problems we do today.

But, we can't say the same for the Leftist "snatch the guns" reactors. They don't see the real issue, Trump does: China.

With an irresponsibly depleted military, the last remaining reason China has not invaded the United States is all the guns at large throughout the country. The 2nd Amendment's militia training of all citizens would solve our gun violence problem, but it's still not satisfactory for national defense. We need a stronger military.

This terrible omnibus budget that Congress sent to Trump makes a mockery of Congress, not Trump. Trump signed it because of its military budget that would make Reagan proud. It's the largest military budget in US history.

Signing the budget will not hurt Trump's changes of re-election. There will be unpopularity for a while, but this showed his "presidential sensibility" and he will have plenty of time to turn this against the dissenters in Congress with them leaving for the 2018 campaign trail. Trump's base will understand him. International threats from a decade of military neglect is the bigger problem we face. Trumpists will blame Congress and many of those laughing at Trump now could find themselves fired in November.

Symphony has long said that mid terms on new presidents often flop as they likely will in 2018. But, mid-term losses will bring out the Conservative vote in 2020 and more voter turnout altogether.

In the economy, Facebook is in trouble, but it will
survive better than the media would have us think.
It's a good time to buy Facebook stock since it's low
—that is with the "buy low, sell high" principle. The
company was also founded and headed by a kid
with little experience. Manipulating news feeds,
suspending accounts, and not planning better for
sneaky operations like Cambridge Analytica—they
were bound for "brat" troubles. But, Facebook is
too important for society to let it slide. The bigger
debate yet to come will be over AI research "big"
money that will want terabytes of user data to
make an AI seem like it has a soul, as part of the
AI cult that thinks Star Trek the Motion Picture is
reality. A takeover by the public under a
combination of stock market status and public
utility laws will be the miraculous solution we will
be told to think was the brilliant answer no one
else thought of.

In another sector of society and politics,
manufacturing is coming back to America. This
will humble and strengthen the United States as it
should. The US will no longer be a "service
economy" where all the other [implied-to-be]
"lesser" nations do the manufacturing and
Americans merely oversee work that is "beneath"
them. By having an equal playing field, Americans
will come down off their pedestal and start doing
hard, skilled labor just like every other nation
needs to do. The two younger hard working
generations are returning not only to political

involvement, but also entrepreneurship and good, old fashioned hard work.

Cadence of Conflict: Asia, March 26

China has out-shined. In the game of power, that's an execution wish. With an aging population, an irritated neighborhood, a loudly whining generation of kids in Hong Kong drawing media attention, and the taste of freedom provided by trade with the outside world, China's Communist party is trouble where the West is concerned.

China's ruling party has not courted support from any territory either under its control or that it aspires to control. Some old school idealists in the retiring generation will support old empire methods, but they aren't the muscle of the future. The gray-head Communists who dye their hair black don't understand what a mess adult children can make when someone takes away their toys because that never happened in China before. Allowing their people to do business with the West injected those Western ideals and China can't go back.

Now, with the massive assertions of power in China, those assertions are about to get stronger. Watch for greater power grabs by the Communist Party. But, even with the power grabs of recent weeks, the rest of the world—including Asia and the West—is on high alert. Russia's only interest in China is to disrupt the rest of the West, not to have a new rival that changes as fast as Beijing does, in its own back yard of all places. These tariffs from the US and Trump signing a pro-military and otherwise Liberal omnibus spending bill from Congress indicate American resolve to halt China in its tracks—at least the Communists.

As for the ongoing "freedom of navigation" sail-bys in the poetically appropriately named Mischief Reef, Britain is also on board, as it were. The US just did another this week with the USS Mustin. China reacted in predictable anger as if on cue.

So, the assault against China's Communism has begun. The West think they can win by using rage to control the "bull in the China shop", as the saying goes. All it would take is one, small Western ship being disrupted by the Chinese and the fury of America's democracy would stand up—with the greatest military budget in history already approved for the next two years.

Encore of Revival: America, April 2

Washington is moving against corporate giants. Gear up.

David Hogg is under ad hominem character assassination from multiple directions. He curses and is disrespectful. He advocates action to be quick and to stop deliberating, not removing the 2nd Amendment. Other anti-2nd Amendment students are being conflated with Hogg's position. The reason for this partial Right Wing, mad-dog assault on David's character is unknown, except that he is the loudest and easiest target while people in close social proximity to him are Leftists. It should be the other Leftists, not David Hogg, that the Right Wing should focus on.

The anti-ad attack against Laura Ingraham would normally fail, except that she's wrong; colleges are just stupid much of the time. She seemed to be part of a mindless Right Wing attack against David because her defense of bureaucratic colleges is rare form. This seems very unlike the Conservative media. Her apology seemed more like a cave-in and demonstrated that she doesn't really have a direction. The apology didn't do any good since advertisers pulled anyway. The lesson here is two-fold: 1. Ingraham should have stuck to her statement, no matter how silly, expounded on the whole situation—not apologized—, and thus at least gained a sense of direction. 2. Never apologize when a hypocritical media asks you to. Public apologies for statements in the media have now proven to be permanently useless.

The Christian concept of an apology is forgiveness. Suddenly, Mark Zuckerberg took this approach, indicating that he may have a moral center after all, even with Facebook's censorship of some accounts. Jesus taught us to love our enemies and to give justice to everyone; silencing "bad people" isn't justice to everyone. If someone is bad, the Facebook community of users should see why. If Facebook censors an account it should be for posting incriminating content only. But, the people who demand apologies want admission of guilt, not restoration, because they are part of an anti-Christian attack on everything good in this world. This week, the Right Wing got caught up in the mindless mob-think in attacking David Hogg's character.

This means one thing: The People's Party is coming.

Stormy Daniels is promoting her story in a way that makes perfect sense if her goal is to get media attention. Her story could be true or false and this "marketing" method would still hold true. Lawyers promote her interviews as one would a movie. They talk about money. She promotes her social media connections. And, she has commented that her bookings are up. It's just interesting how much business she has gotten from this and it will be more interesting to see how it pans out.

There is a gross contradiction, however, with Stormy Daniels and the Left. Being a porn star, she is hardly a moral judge. More importantly, the Left Wing did not attack Bill Clinton anywhere near as much.

Cadence of Conflict: Asia, April 2

China and the US have fixed their rudders on a ramming course. The only remaining question will be over whose hull is stronger.

The "yuge" US trade deficit with China is purported to be $375B USD. Bloomberg was sure to point out that the figure is inflated, some way or another. Xinhua news reports that a more accurate figure is a mere $298B USD deficit. Trump sent a "Section 301" notice of unfair trade tactics to China along with $50–60B USD in tariffs, depending on which news source you read. Trump also asked China to reduce the deficit by a whopping $100B USD and China says that the US is being unfair, placing tariffs on US food.

Asian markets are up, but a Caixin market index— something like a DOW Jones average in China— isn't up as much as hoped. Everyone has an opinion on what all that means.

Companies in America believe that tariffs harm the consumer. Some voices argue that the US has a "service" trade surplus with China, but still a deficit overall. Trump argues that trade deficits harm the worker and the overall economy. Basic macro-economic theory would say that workers would afford higher prices with much higher pay.

Trade deficits initiated the Opium Wars with China when China welcomed a one-way flow of silver from Britain for tea, but would not allow the eager Chinese population to import British goods. The Opium Wars ended with surrender of several lands to Britain, including Hong Kong. China's current and main land dispute is over Taiwan. The stage is set for history to repeat and so far it has.

Taiwan is certainly chumming up to the US as China attempts to endear the Taiwanese. Most recently, Taiwan is buying more advanced missiles from the US while two Senators advocate selling F-35s to Taiwan—a sale more likely since Taiwan's current administration is unlikely to set up secret talks with China as the rival party attempted nearly four years ago. China banned Taiwanese movies casting a purportedly pro-independence Taiwanese actor, Lawrence Ko.

Encore of Revival: America, April 9

America is unquestionably in a culture war. The two Black ladies, Diamond and Silk, are "unsafe to the community" according to Facebook. That might have been the last straw. Many people in America love those two women and will take Facebook's opinion personally. It does have logical implications: If you like someone who is "unsafe to the community" then it stands to reason that you too are "unsafe". After all, if you want to see Diamond and Silk videos in your feed then Facebook disagrees with you.

But, that's not where it stopped.

Tony Robins, a pioneer in his field of encouraging people with self-motivation, has helped many people make better lives for themselves. He commented that using a hashtag on Twitter to feel good merely uses a drug called "significance". People who clean up their lives have already come to teach themselves that being famous and harming someone else offer no improvement for quality of life. And, indeed, the "womens rights" movement is no exception—just like Christianity— in having been abused by people who just want to feel good by way of fame. Tony Robins did not disrespect the "MeToo" movement, but only called-out the human habit of using good things for an alternative purpose.

Then, a woman in the audience proved his point for him by contorting his defense of personal responsibility into something it was not.

False alarms diminish the value of the alarm. America needs an uprising of people who will not stay quiet in the face of abuse. Tony Robins identified a new, niche form of abuse as a warning against crying "victim" in excess. Alienating Tony will not hurt Tony, it will hurt the groupies who commandeered the genuine, real call to end degradation of women.

With a march on the way to the border and the military being called into question, America faces turbulence, but these things will not overcome the nation; they will purge the problems and make the nation stronger.

Cadence of Conflict: Asia, April 9

China has been a source of great change.

Taiwan has received a license from the United States to build its own submarines. Wang, a legislature who sits on the Foreign Affairs and National Defense Committee said that friendliness from the US is the highest it has ever been. Japan just commissioned its first marine force since WWII. 1,500 troops are ready, specifically to repel invasion of Japan's islands. Thanks to China's inspiration and initiative, many nations in the region are also making their contribution to peace and stability in Pacific Asia.

The US is re-evaluating trade with China. While much is just talk, Trump maintains friendly rhetoric. The shakeup with trade will force countries to reinvent and reevaluate trade policy. While a looming "trade war" remains the talk of many so-called "experts", the long-term benefit will be the overall rebirth of trade throughout the world. Everyone will need to rethink trade. Any kind of thinking is good, especially in these times.

Encore of Revival: America, April 16

The self-destructive establishmentarians are imploding the FBI from the helm and Facebook is run by kids who don't know what they're doing.

For decades the FBI was considered above reproach, but not anymore. Raiding a private attorney's office and private residence stoops to new lows after an investigation has only proven less and less likely to find a problem. It proved more unlikely after this raid. The real purpose of the raid was to punish Cohen for being Trump's attorney to discourage others from working with the president who is draining the establishment's swamp. Now, that swamp is making it evident why it must be drained.

Trump should not fire Mueller; he should suspend his work and his team while a special council is hired to investigate what went on in a special counsel investigation team that hasn't found anything since it was commissioned.

Facebook's kids at the helm understand computer code and know how to make software, but like the kids running most app companies, they don't have the scruples to guide their software to make just and fair decisions for their users. We see the child-like culture in Zuckerberg's apology to the public and how he pleads with the Senate committee members like a child asking to keep the keys to his car.

The best explanation of Comey is fear that Clinton would get elected and retaliate if he tried to harm her or didn't help her before her election. He expected her election, which holds bearing on his decisions. This "higher road" approach is often used by politically-oriented and otherwise incompetent leaders who appear pious as they refuse to pursue justice against those who harm others. He didn't want to be "the torture guy" and he didn't want to go after Clinton; nice guys don't do those things, after all.

Cadence of Conflict: Asia, April 16

The war with China is becoming the war with Russia and China, it's economic, it's culminating, and Britain is double-involved.

Since the strike on Syria, Russia is angry and thumping the drums. They promised retaliation before. After, they really promised really retaliation next time. It almost seems that Trump is testing Russian and Chinese leadership—and North Korea and Republican and Democrat—and has called their bluff. That's coming at the US via Europe. But, Germany is also taking rhetorical shots at China, bringing Europe back into the Pacific conflict.

Britain is in contemplating trade talks with Taiwan. The UK is already involved in the Pacific conflict with Hong Kong's exit status—that China will have no involvement in Hong Kong matters for fifty years as a condition of Hong Kong not being British. With Britain "friending" up to Taiwan, we see more involvement from the Crown.

But, the main fuel in the Pacific conflict is economics. US sanctions are successfully driving Kim to the table; China is eager to work with Japan before a Kim-Trump talk disarms the North. So, the US sanctions are also driving China and Japan to do at least something.

Then, there's China's own economics. Germany is
angry about Chinese investments in Europe. More
news stories this week talk of Chinese using money
as a hostile takeover tool in Sri Lanka and
Pakistan. China's ability to stand against a US
trade war goes back to US Treasury bonds and the
direct devaluing of China's own currency. While
different "experts" have differing opinions, money
is the talk—everywhere.

Encore of Revival: America, April 23

Grandpa Giuliani is starring as Marc Antony to end the conflict and save the country from a divisive justice fled to brutish beats from men who have lost their reason. The former mayor is in a position to bring such a resolution. The New York district doing the FBI investigation knows him, his city knows him, the nation knows him, the investigator knows him, the president knows him. He knows everyone in the family as does any grandpa know his own.

Rudy Giuliani has the impeccable credentials Mueller was said to have had before his year-long investigation made wary everyone with any opinion. No one could threaten him, no one would have any cause to investigate him since he has been distant all this time. To investigate Giuliani at this point would beg the same question the Russian attorney is asking: Why hasn't someone at least interviewed me?

No doubt, the shrinking number of investigation supporters will say, "Trump's old pal Rudi got him out of it." But, that won't help their cause and the investigation will end nonetheless.

As anti-Trump sentiment both shrinks and honkers-down, many are getting fed up, especially with the Starbucks overreaction and now Amazon's ratings about ratings. Closing thousands of locations for "racial bias" training will backfire; it's only theater. If Starbucks really cares about solving the problem of "implicit" biases, they would keep their doors open to customers, pay staff to come in early, and train them in smaller groups during breaks over multiple sessions. People know it's useless, both Leftists and Conservatives, employees and customers. This drama, combined with the overreaction of protesters shouting at Starbucks employees who agree with them will only drive more people to support Trump.

After all, a vote for Trump is really a way of protesting protests.

Then, we have Comey's book on Amazon. Mashable and the Verge credit Deadline for breaking the story just before 9 p.m. on Friday, which a Rush Limbaugh caller, Chris, mentioned prior to 2 p.m. that same day. Gizmodo mentions that negative reviews won't be possible from Trump supporters. Generally absent from mainstream articles are any exploration of the idea that phony positive reviews are also disallowed and could be a part of rating fraud or bias. Many also note the same information, that Amazon has blocked non-customer ratings on potentially controversial books in the past.

What we know about Amazon's block on ratings is an absence of negative reviews and Amazon's own claim that there appears to be some sort of bias from ratings. Everything real receives good and bad ratings alike. After this, Amazon's reviews will likely lose credibility.

With the Starbucks overreaction and now Amazon claiming that its own rating system of Comey's new book is in question, we could be looking at such a surge of new Trump voters that 2018 actually sees a boost in the Republican victories in the House and Senate. But, things are so wild and goofy these days that we can't make heads or tails of what is going on politically. The swamp is being drained and, in any foreseeable case, Trump will almost certainly win again in 2020 and we are staring down the road of a future Republican Supreme Court.

Trump's appointee to the Supreme Court, Justice Neil Gorsuch, voted against action that would normally favor Trump's campaign platform to fix immigration. The ruling, however, was not about politics, but about sloppily-written law. We need laws to be written better and we need a Supreme Court that thinks so.

Barbara Bush passed away last week at the age of 92. She was mourned by friends, family, and all living past presidents.

Cadence of Conflict: Asia, April 23

The US is arming East Asia and disarming North Korea. China is a spectator in the Western game.

Reports and gossip about the latest North Korean promise to disarm ensnared many in the media. The South Korean Kumbaya singing President Moon Jae-in was quick to give his "peace in our time" report that North Korea has promised to disarm, with the connotatively-added meaning of "shortly after his election". Trump Tweeted that disarming is great, "yuge" news, then the mainstream media ripped on Trump for an unverified report, particularly PBS. (Why does PBS still receive tax dollar money?) Japan's Prime Minister Shinzo Abe was more cautions about North Korean false promises, proving himself the most sober in the room.

Japan is looking into a stealthy F-22 F-35 hybrid from Lockheed Martin, in order to deter impedance from "Chinese" and "Russian" jets in its air defense zone. Taiwan is also looking at Patriot missile defense systems. The increased military talk in China's backyard, particularly about China, surmounts to the dogs fighting over who gets to eat the pheasant.

China is making so many flybys around Taiwan that scrambling jets over air defense zone approaches is a strain on the Taiwanese military budget. Taiwan might end up sending China a bill, likely by way of military money from the US and US tariffs on not yet mentioned Chinese goods. Also look for new Taiwan-favored trade deficits with the US in amounts similar to the cost of scrambling jets every few days.

Encore of Revival: America, April 30

Immigration is at the top of everything—news, speeches, law enforcement...

Building contractors hoping to get the contract for the Trump wall should be very pleased with this caravan of immigrants just arriving at the border, as should the Republican Party. With the failing Russianewsgategate investigation from Mueller, this immigrant caravan has almost guaranteed a contrary-to-the-norm Republican pickup in the 2018 election. Trump even knows that he can threaten to shut down the government to build the wall just before an election.

The interesting part of this caravan—as well as other illegal immigrant crackdown new stories—is that the caravan may actually believe that their journey will have the reverse affect that it's having. And, the news media also seems to think that reporting on illegal immigration crackdowns will make the public think that immigration is less of a problem. Perhaps the media and the marchers live in the same world. It makes sense since experience in one subculture can cause the reality of another subculture to become counterintuitive.

Cadence of Conflict: Asia, April 30

One easy way to understand, at most "anticipate," but at least be unsurprised by developments in Korea and China is the "PDT Symphony Mad Asian Scientist Theorem". This "Mad Scientist" theorem is not fact and likely untrue, but if applied, events somehow make sense. The theorem is as follows.

Let's say there is a mad scientist somewhere in Asia who freely travels between China and North Korea. He studies a very specific niche: civilian control. Over the last sixty years or so, he would have easily observed in North Korea what happens to a society with absolute police state control over a comparatively small population completely isolated from the outside world. Propaganda and behavior are equally managed and controlled by the government there. This hypothetical "mad scientist" would have all the information he needs to understand an Orwellian society in full swing.

Then, let's say, for whatever reason, North Korea is no longer a viable source for his societal studies and experiments—however he manages to implement them. He then goes to China, which seems to be following the same Orwellian methods, but on a population fifty times larger. That is the theorem.

As North Korea stops being the perfect place for
the mythical "mad scientist", China suddenly
becomes the new laboratory. It's not actually
happening that way; it just seems to be. One small
example of this is China's new use of facial
recognition; police wearing face-recognition
glasses, face-recognition police robots looking for
bad guys at train stations, and even cameras using
face-recognition to crack down on the great threat
of J-walking. No question, China is the world's new
North Korea, but with tech the Kim Dynasty never
dreamed of.

Whatever is going on behind the scenes, this
"peace deal" with North Korea is not all that it is
purported or reported to be. South Koreans will be
led to believe that the new peace will be the result
of the new president Moon Jae-in's emphasis on
"diplomacy". However much his diplomacy may
have in fact helped, it's not just any old kind of
diplomacy. Obama also stressed diplomacy and we
saw what happened there—or better said what
didn't happen. South Korea's president had a
special diplomacy, but he hasn't said what made
his so diplomatic methods get actual results.

Just as much, Trump's embargo against North
Korea also stepped up pressure, something obvious
that receives some mention, but not much mention
because it's so obvious. The more likely Trump-
effected factor in the North Korean deal is China.
That you are likely to hear little about from Trump
since people who make a difference rarely share all
of their trade secrets. Trump is the great deal

maker, after all. So, there is no way that we will know what all went on behind the scenes.

What most likely happened was a US implied threat made to China, a simple reveal of US military capability. "China, back off or you're boiled toast, cooked, and well-done." That's what kind of message China must have gotten, one way or another. This is all the more obvious because of China's response, grasping for friends.

Even with all this bravado about playing hardball with the US, China just opened up foreign investments at warp speed. Of course, China loves it when foreign money flows one-way into its markets. It's working with an economic team from the US. And, China is also working on economics with its old, hard-earned enemy India—in the same "bromance" as Xi had with Trump.

The India deal won't work because China always negotiates with a factor of "saving face", an brittle value. If China really wanted India's friendship, it would apologize for all past disputes—whether right or wrong—and permanently surrender all disputed land to India. But, it won't because China isn't demonstrating any change of heart, only a state of desperation.

For China's sake, the decision makers in Beijing must be careful. India is no fool and "desperate" is exactly what India will see. India's president will seek to exploit as much as he can from China, but India is by no means a friend of a nation that

wants to be friendly and save face at the same
time.

Encore of Revival: America, May 7

The leaked questions Mueller would ask Trump should raise eyebrows about how deep the Russianewsgategate theatrics go. Contrary to propaganda, the grammatical errors don't indicate that the list came from Trump because Trump uses very accurate grammar. For example, when most people would say, "They did bad," Trump often says this correctly, "They did badly." Interestingly, the "bad grammar" notion about Trump is a pop culture superstition stirred by the press among people who actually do have bad grammar. This coupled with the "bad grammar" argument coming from Mueller's side of this lynch attempt indicates that the same people promoting the "bad grammar" view of Trump could also likely be behind this framing. Moreover, a "bad grammar" list makes the list more likely authentic, as if it is a collection of small notes of incomplete sentences that an interviewer would refer to when asking the real questions, of course with correct grammar.

Trump's nonchalant disappointment in the Russianewsgategate investigation indicates that Trump has turned this into a war of legs rather than a war of arms; he intends to let it drag on until it loses all steam and the nation is tired of it —both his supporters tired from the pettiness and his opponents tired from results not delivered.

The Leftist arm of the mass media is certainly helping Trump. The most recent fake news about Cohen's phone having been tapped—reported by NBC, reiterated by CNBC—is just the latest example. It's almost as if they are trying to give Trump easy excuses to discredit them.

Another strange aspect of the Russianewsgategate "collusion" myth is the gross contradiction: With all the love and adoration that the Leftist arm of the media has held for Russia, with the Clintons having warm relations with Russia, the same media should be glad if they believe that Trump is working with their Russian role models of economics and leadership. But, they aren't happy about the prospect of Trump cooperating with Russia because they don't believe it's true. This is just a ruse to connect Trump to the Hollywood myth of the "usual RAVs"—"Russians, Arabs, and Villans". They were hoping that the American public would buy it.

Or were they? If we interpret the actions of the Leftist arm of the media, it seems they throw one slow ball after another so Trump can keep whacking it out of the park. Anti-Trumpists have no reason to be pleased with the Anti-Trump effort from the Leftists media sources they occasionally watch. It looks more and more like the Symphony opinion was right: 2018 could see an uptick in Republican victories—not that the Republican establishment can be trusted, but that times are certainly changing, something uncreative leaders in entrenched establishments loath.

Cadence of Conflict: Asia, May 7

This was week of talk. A delegation from Washington went to talk with China. Trump talked about talking nice while talking. Economic talking heads are talking about the talks and everybody's talking about it. Once the delegation that went to Beijing to talk gets back, they will talk with Trump. Warren Buffet even had some things to talk about.

Trump's delegation to Beijing was indeed an olive branch. It spelled out "the line" in the sand, toured it, explained, it, discussed it, explored it, and made that line very, very clear. To quote Morgan Freeman's Lucius Fox, "Mr. Wayne didn't want you to think that he was deliberately wasting your time." But, the line is not the least bit likely to be respected.

China will ignore everything the US delegation explained and forewarned, but they will never be surprised when Trump does exactly what the delegation said he would, though they may act like it. More importantly, the list of expectations shows how well Trump knows China and Chinese methods of doing "business".

Words like "retaliate" and "oppose" often surface with disfavor, as well as the US clearly being wise to the tactic of unofficially using backdoor channels to unofficially impose other restrictions to get what one wants. And, the US maintains its position on the "301" trade notice that China is non-market economy, specifically that China is to drop the matter completely and withdraw its appeals on the matter with the WTO.

There is no wiggle room in the US demands and those demands strongly demonstrate that Trump knows exactly the kinds of things Chins is likely to do. In essence the list of demands forbids exactly what China is most likely to do in the near future.

By contrast, China's demands are mainly that the US back off on its recent action; that's all. Consider the argument going around from pro-China stories about the trade "imbalance"—especially that US's service and consulting help to narrow the "trade deficit". The list of Chinese demands don't account for this or ask that they be calculated in the "trade deficit".

The mere demands, in themselves, tell us that China does not know what is about to happen in Washington and that Trump knows all to well—probably better than any of his advisers in the White House—what will happen in Beijing. China is in great danger.

Surprises are coming, somewhere. That's how history always plays out. No war ends without the unexpected and there's always a joker or two hiding in the deck. The surprises will likely include special and disputed territories, such as Macau, Hong Kong, and Taiwan, as well as international public opinion and some sector of trade or international protocol not yet considered or discussed by anyone—they will surprise everyone. That "surprise sector" could include ocean boundaries or specific products often traded. It could also be an act of God, such as an earthquake, hurricane, or tsunami. But, we have no idea except that any intermediate history student should anticipate at least two surprises before the current cloud passes in the greater storm.

China looks at the US the way the poor working class looked at the aristocracy in Russia. Beijing thinks they are demanding "what is their right". Remember, this is akin to "Opium War III", started by a trade imbalance. China demands that the money and "tax payable by way of free technology" continue to flow net into China; the US demands things like "equal" and "fair" in the flow. That is rhetoric from the Opium War prelude. If that war resurfaces, the "English" speaking country won't be Britain, though Britain still has a dog in the fight: Hong Kong is not to be changed for fifty years, yet this week Hong Kong military youth groups—comparable to Boy Scouts—rejected Chinese requests that they march according to PLA marching steps—meaning that China tried to make a change and Hong Kong could become a target for punitive action from China. Hence, Hong Kong is "fair play" in everyone's opinion, including public opinion about everyone in the game.

If China had any kind of conflict with the West—whether militarily or over trade—the conclusion could require complete surrender of Hong Kong back to British rule—and Hong Kongers wouldn't mind.

In the territorial disputes, Taiwan declaring independence would certainly rock the boat. Research says Taiwanese overwhelmingly view China as unfriendly. So, Taiwanese certainly wouldn't mind making their contribution to making a few waves.

China is already on the bench with the Korean issue. Pyongyang just updated the North clocks to no longer be thirty minutes off, but back in time with the South. Where's China?—exchanging trade demands with the country whose trade blockade preceded the Korean talks.

In all this, Warren Buffet's advice is that China is a good place for the West to invest. We'll see.

Encore of Revival: America, May 14

Trump rescinding the so-called "Iran deal" will improve his position with other nations, North Korea only being one of them. Actually, it wasn't a "deal" because Iran never signed anything.

Any "reputation" lost would be on Iran's side for entering into a "deal" that even they didn't commit to. Now the non-committal "deal" is off. Iran shouldn't have expected anything. Now, at the bargaining table, Trump will be in a better position because nations know that he will actually follow through and only make deals that are real and binding.

This goes back to Obama's great failure of his own base: He didn't make laws that would last, he only made policies that depend on him being president in order to last, in this he exploited his voters by giving them high hopes and letting them get angry —the whole time Obama never told his own supporters the truth that everything he accomplished after Obamacare was designed to be blown away with the wind.

Iranians weren't the only party with "gullible" written their foreheads; Obama voters were too, and Obama conned all of them.

The disturbing thing about the Iran "deal" is the reaction. Russia is very protective of that "deal". That should be enough to call the "deal" off—and to prove that there was no substance in the Russianewsgategate "collusion" myth. But, where are all the stories in the press about how the "deal" was bad for the US? Having given $1.7B in cash to Iran should at least receive mention from a supposed "non-biased" media.

Cadence of Conflict: Asia, May 14

Disassembling nuke sites prior to meeting Trump may seem like a "save of face" for Kim Jong-Un, but it's actually a statement of Trump's influence. If Trump wasn't an influence, then Kim wouldn't be doing what Trump has been demanding for a long time. No doubt, North Korea and its pro-Communist supporters in the Liberal media will twist this into "Trump not making a difference" from Trump getting what he wanted even before a meeting.

The comparison from history would be a feudal lord quickly accomplishing everything his king asked before his next royal visit. To say the king didn't make a difference would be just plain ignorant. We should expect as much.

But, Trump wants it that way. The more Trump has his name on the Korean reunification, the more China's desperate thirst for "respect" will sting. China wants everything to look like everything everywhere was China's idea, or else throw a temper tantrum. Trump's low-key silence will deny the "fight fix" and the semi-centennial tantrum will have to wait a little longer.

Encore of Revival: America, May 21

Call it a Shame of Thrones or a Game of Showns, but Mueller has shown his game to his own shame. By waiting as long as he has, Trump possesses the "political currency" to order the DOJ to investigate the Obama FBI. He couldn't have done that a year ago. But, by letting Mueller "mull" on, as it were, the Russianewsgategate "thing" has irritated everyone, even the Anti-Trumpists, for its lack of results, yet continued pursuit in what looks more and more like a ghost chase every day—now every hour.

Roger Stone says Trump might not run in the next term—if he gets his [twelve years worth of] work done in only four. With Democrats requiring 84 days to approve each of 300 Trump appointees, it's unlikely Trump will finish in four years, as Stone's hypothetical went. Michael Jordan said the same thing about himself year after year, that he might not play the following season—encouraging his opponents to get lazy. It's a ruse Trump opponents would be foolish to buy into. If the Democrats really wanted Trump to not run again, they would approve all his Senate appointees and build his wall in one vote. Then, it would be difficult for Trump to argue any need to stay, even with such "huge" results.

The Senate's vote on net neutrality is a necessary step. Internet needs some kind of regulation, even if to say that it needs no regulation, even if to protect it from anti-Capitalist corptocrats who donate to "Blue Dog Republicans". If Facebook and Google want to provide faster Internet then they can become their own Internet service providers. If Verizon wants to say which big, fat companies can "pay for lane" in the website rat race, then Verizon should provide that Internet service free of charge. But, as long as customers pay, those customers should get to decide the lanes. This is not to be decided by Verizon, AT&T, Facebook, Google, Apple, and other big, fat companies that have more money than many governments of the world. Capitalism does not infer that private companies should overrule human rights.

Cadence of Conflict: Asia, May 21

Talk only went so far this week. I looks as if North Korea might not be dismantling its nukes, but hiding them, then threatening to close talks when exposed for this, then threatening to cancel the summit for some other list of excuses.

The big question on Kim Jong-Un backing out on the talks relates to his recent visits to China. Not that China has made any wild promises, but he feels somewhat confident in getting lippy with the US.

The big lesson was about Moon's emphasis on diplomacy vs Trump's emphasis on teeth. Diplomacy made progress in terms of leading to more diplomacy. But, actual action is a measurement of its own. So far, Trump's action has led to China losing interest in any kind of trade war and Moon's favored diplomacy seems to be leading to an undiplomatic end to diplomacy.

Things aren't over nor have we seen the last surprise. The big news of the week is that China's on the bench. Moon and Trump will meet to discuss Kim having a discussion with them in Singapore. Where's China?—announcing its surrender on trade, reflecting on past meetings with Kim, another player that doesn't really matter.

If Kim doesn't show up, Moon's populist diplomacy
will prove to have failed and Trump will have the
"political currency" for action against North Korea.
Maybe that's what China hopes for in allowing Kim
to gain false hopes in something or other—to
rationalize a little retaliatory action of its own. But,
if military action was China's first preference,
Beijing would have already taken it.

Encore of Revival: America, May 28

Charlie Cook now says what Symphony has said for weeks: Republicans look more and more like they are headed for an unusual midterm upswing. The part you won't read is how much it looks like a Democrat conspiracy to get Republicans elected—because, if reverse psychology were the plan, Democrats played every note on cue and in key. There's no evidence of this at all, other than how incredibly flawless the execution seems to be. Either it is a conspiracy for some crazy cause or the current Democrats in office are just as stupid as the Republicans during Bush's second term.

The general political trend over the weekend was the correlation between society and meteorology. The day after a civil protest occurs, the weather goes nutso. If the government "zaps" publication of the courts, lightning strikes sixty thousand times. If a mob floods the streets one day, a flood floods the streets the next. Now, a hurricane is on its way to Florida. Make sure, if you plan to go golfing in the afternoon, don't express any objections outside any government buildings in the morning. Your T-time might get rained on.

Cadence of Conflict: Asia, May 28

The US "disinvited" two countries this week, not only North Korea, but also China from the biannual naval exercises in Hawaii. Both "disinvitations" were a rescinding of a previous invitation after less than friendly saber rattling from the former invitee. Kim Jong Un's loud mouth is widely known, so the North Korean "disinvitation" came as no surprise.

China, specifically, has been pressuring African countries to "dis-recognize" Taiwan in favor of Beijing policy. Additionally, China has been pressuring US companies to follow otherwise unrecognized Chinese maps placing Taiwan under China's political sovereignty, as well as companies from other countries—which Taiwan is not currently under the control of. China sees the request as part of a grand goal of "reunification" and a nostalgic return to the rhapsodic geographical past as the keystone of a socioeconomic strengthening strategy.

The problem from the Western corporate perspective is with the dictionary, not with ideology. China's government does not decide the laws on Taiwan's island currently, not in any way. So, listing Taiwan "under" China would create confusion for Western tourists. But, China is run by Communists who believe that logistics are to be dictated, not recognized. In the land of Communist-Chinese, if tourists would be confused, the solution is to simply make a new law this afternoon outlawing tourists who are confused. So, Beijing doesn't believe the West has any legitimate problem with the policy, but that Western companies are only trying to spite Beijing.

Washington, however, does view the problem as ideological. It would be wrong for Washington to dictate the organizational nomenclature of the Bank of China or Sky News or Spotify. So would be any reciprocal resemblance. Under Trump, Washington is enforcing that ideology globally.

Then, there was yet another snafu among China's man-made islands. The US can't stop making news in Taiwan. A Senator makes an "unexpected" visit. US weapons developers are planning to set up shop in Taiwan. The US and Taiwan have decided that they can't build Taiwanese submarines fast enough. And, the US has decided that Taiwan needs the absolutely best defense to respond to Chinese "saber rattling", not only asymmetric defense. All of this is remarkably irritating and "disrespectful" to China.

China hates few things more than being disrespected.

Encore of Revival: America, June 4

Trey Gowdy's act is over. Over the years he made many statements that any novice analyst could predict would draw respect from normal America. Now, he supports the FBI, against the instincts of his hard-earned supporters, without having read up on what he's talking about? Perhaps the whole time he ran on instinct and just got lucky. Nearing retirement, his lucky streak is running out. Perhaps he should just retire altogether and quit while he's ahead. He's already done so much that he could make a bigger difference from Twitter, on the condition that he reads up in advance and stays on his game like Rudy Giuliani.

Giuliani has some of the best and most-common sense advice about Russianewsgategate: No interview without seeing the evidence first. That's just, plain normal practice. Rudy's statement is a warning shot across Mueller's bow, specifically that Rudy is neither fool nor pushover, not to mention that Mueller has already gone out of bounds by not offering that evidence prior to seeking an interview. So-called "experts" and other political pundits should be able to figure out by now that Trump is bulletproof. The good news for the country is that Giuliani is achieving his mission, even against the current; he's bringing the Russianewsgategate scandal to a peaceful halt.

The cancellation of Rosanne is abominable—not because of the political alignments, but because of the "always cave-in" cowardice mode of operation in corptocratic America. Rosanne Barr deserves a purple heart and a medal of honor in the social world. People make regrettable remarks, whether we say what we don't really think or we blurt whatever we think when we might should keep it to ourselves. It is the fool who dost not forgive.

ABC and Disney just trashed one of the most shining gems in their own industry, from within their own collection. The lead actress exercised the same kind of free speech and vocabulary that the Left use every day, and the industry giants shut down one of their own best-viewed shows in history, unemploying the cast, and vanishing its viewers. That doesn't make math. If Rosanne Barr was in violation of any contract, she should have been fined. This compares to shooting helpless hostages when the scientist won't dance to the furer's demands. So, ABC and Disney have set the precedent in the entertainment establishment: If you are part of a show, you're being held hostage as the escape goat should someone else get out of line with the party.

In light of the less-so-silent majority, Rosanne Barr could be the most employable woman in growing Conservative America.

Cadence of Conflict: Asia, June 4

North Korea inches further and further toward talks with the US. China fears this. If Kim Jong-Un get in the same room as the man who wrote The Art of the Deal, North Korea could become a stronger ally to the US than even South Korea overnight. That would likely lead to a quick reunification of the Korean Peninsula, as well as other shifts in power, even before any alliance might be formalized. But, Trump's deal-making reputation should bring no shocks to what is about to transpire in the Singapore Summit.

Then, there's China, about to be left behind. The hardline crackdown on free speech throughout China won't be without consequence. Symphony has been saying so for years; Albert Ho effectively said the same, quoted in a Bloomberg article dated June 4. Party power is getting brittle. But, the consequences of brutal brittality are rarely explored. So, here goes.

Hong Kong won't shut up anytime soon. The whining, whimpering bratty students of Hong Kong may be wrong to demand rights when freedom was largely handed to them by the British. But, those bratty students sure are drawing a press load of attention to China. That alone should be a heavy factor in logistics calculation. Hong Kong is a megaphone for any anti-China sentiment because the world reads about Hong Kong every day. After all, Hong Kong is "Asia's World City".

But, then there's the problem of cracking down within "China proper", the Mainland governed directly by Beijing, not a SAR like Hong Kong or Macau. If China considers friendly sarcasm to be a threat within China—that means tech companies and hardware manufacturers won't have candid conversations about quality control and competitive design. Once free speech becomes a minefield, people will divert mental resources away from fee and open brainstorming toward making sure that they don't say anything offensive. The key to good brainstorm sessions and innovation is that nothing is off the table and no one is allowed to take offense at anything whatsoever. That's can't happen in China anymore. Bye-bye Western manufacturing paradise. It's only a matter of time before Western outsourcing brands figure it out. One little story, like an innovator being locked up for a tech suggestion because it was interpreted as "opposing to the Party", might plunge Chinese factory stocks into the void below.

"Single-Party Rule" is the key topic now, at least according to Western papers. That's the protest mantra in Hong Kong. It's the talking point of headlines and marches. It is the so-called "problem" as is being presented to the world. The Western press is on a path for reporting a narrative that stirs sentiment for two-party rule in China. Whether it's a typhoon, an earthquake, a solar flare, or some other "act of God", if China suddenly adopts a two-party system, Western newspaper readers will have already been prepped to think it is a good thing.

Then, there's Vietnam, exploring foreign investment "zones". Deserved or unfair, distrust is stirring against China as a place of investment. This will have a double-edged effect in Vietnam. Firstly, Western manufacturing will flock to Vietnam as a way of fleeing the newspaper villain, China. But, with a Communist Party having total rule in Vietnam, Western investors will demand certain assurances before dumping too much money into yet another single-party market. Sooner or later, we could be looking at Vietnam adopting a friendly two-party system as a stronger strategy of competing with China. That will only add to the momentum of change in East Asia.

Encore of Revival: America, June 11

Reciprocal trade is the trend of everyone. Canada charges 270% tariffs on US dairy in the midst of the NAFTA "free trade" agreement, Trump threatens to charge other tariffs if trade isn't even, and Trudeau objects to reciprocal tariffs and threatens them at the same summit. If the results were allowed to speak for themselves, it would be hard to know if anyone wants free trade or reciprocal tariffs or if people just want to argue. But, the results aren't in yet. Until they are, we don't know.

Trump left a G7 summit, wishing it were a G8 summit to include Russia, making it a G6 summit while he left for his own G2 summit in Singapore with Kim Jong-Un. Trump solidified the certainty of that summit by canceling it. Reciprocal trade will almost surely be on the shelf. The Western press can't not speculate, especially with the old wives tale that investment is the primary source of economic stimulation—generally overlooking hard work, balancing free markets with regulation, and ingenuity.

The reason Russia is not at the G 7/8 summit is because it took back Crimea via referendum. Khrushchev gave Crimea to the Ukraine in 1954, which was a controversy all to its own. The Obama administration's response was to alienate Russia. Russia's main faux pas in the recovery of Crimea was flying its Russian flag over a government building taken by Russian soldiers prior to the referendum, but that received little attention. The West's opinion at the time was largely limited to who should own what territory in Ukraine and Russia.

Amazon is listening and respecting the religious needs of its Muslim workers in the Twin Cities. Fasting is hot work and the Muslim immigrants need a cooler, slower-paced work environment during Ramadan. No word in the news, however, on reciprocal trade working conditions, such as whether Amazon has negotiated for disposable barbecue celebrations for Taoists on Chinese holidays or fish Friday for Catholics who have so generously immigrated to Muslim countries.

Talk show news punetdom is losing, in life, a lion of the mind, Charles Krauthammer. When the other talking heads from the Potomac beltway and NPR niggled over opinions of the press and heads of state, Krauthammer explained the three step process of delivering a nuclear weapon and where Kim Jong-Il had made progress within those steps. He resented terms like "Washington establishment" and also objected to Trump for fighting against an establishment he deemed mythical. He represented a sobering voice of reason and calm, disagreed with almost everyone about something, politely held to his own opinions, and remained courteous in discussion. He shared a letter within the past

few days that cancer is ending his life and he has
only weeks to live. The world of ideas and politics
already misses him.

Cadence of Conflict: Asia, June 11

The historians and experts are all hysterical about the historic meeting between Trump and Kim. They warn that JFK appeared too week while Nixon's aggression didn't intimidate. No one can win in the eyes of the hindsight expert who sees himself as the smartest guy in the room. But, history has already been made: Trump brought Warmbier home and Kim to the table. No one has done either before as a sitting president.

For the record, former President Bill Clinton did bring home Lisa Ling's younger sister from North Korea under Kim Jong-Il, but he wasn't president at the time and he wasn't dealing with the same leader. Still, Clinton deserves kudos. Presidents Clinton and Trump should have a victory cigar together at some point.

Kim Jong-Un is a kid who has never known the free world. Though there are rumors of him having attended school as a kid in Europe, it would have been just enough to gain an appetite, not an understanding. Donald J. Trump is an old, wealthy man. With talk of a McDonald's and a Trump resort in North Korea being on Kim's wish list, everyone should expect the conversation to be that of the young kid eagerly asking daddy for gifts. Trump's answer will likely be similar to his response to Senator Feinstein, "Sure we can do that…" with the added, "But, those things aren't given by eternally rich countries since no country is eternally rich. Those things are part of a world culture of people coming in and going out, but your father and grandfather wouldn't let people go in or out. If you just let people go in and out, you can get those things yourself without having to ask me."

In all likelihood, no one has ever told those things to Kim Jong-Un before, not even South Korean President Moon who began the current outreach. Everyone has his role. Moon was the charm, Trump may be the evangelist who delivers the good news no one else could. This meeting is not about a hashed-out, jig-sawed "deal"; it's about the only man in the world with both the power and the words to explain life and love to the only man in the world who can't receive those ideas from anyone else.

As Trump and Kim prepare to meet tomorrow, the main news in the Western press about China is China possibly spying on the Trump-Kim summit, that and flashbacks to Nixon and Mao. The rest focuses on the old script of news in China: economics. The SCO summit includes Kazakhstan, Kyrgyzstan, Uzbekistan, Pakistan, Tajikistan, Russia, China, and India. They basically met to agree that they agree. Clearly, China and its neighborhood is solidifying a stark alliance to contrast morphing alliances in the West—and the West's growing alliance with some nations to China's east.

Encore of Revival: America, June 18

The meeting between Kim and Trump has been twisted into a bet over Iran. Canada and Iran believe Obama's Iran deal is the model. They are staking their reputations of knowing what kind of deals lead where in the fate of the Kim-Trump summit. The results will speak for themselves.

In the aftermath of Summit Kim-Trump, Trumpists see the glass as 3/4 full while while Anti-Trumpists see the glass as 3/4 empty. No sitting president has met with the leader of North Korea and received concessions. The Iran deal was arguably as bad as Anti-Trumpists claim Kim-Trump was, and Iran involved cash payments while Kim-Trump did not. The only conclusion we can draw is that people support whomever they already support, our favorites can do no wrong and our disfavored can do nothing right.

Now, Giuliani is calling for an investigation of the investigators. There used to be a department in the federal government that did that. It was called the FBI until Comey got involved. But, those days are behind us.

The US is polarizing, but the poles are also shifting.

Some LGBTQAYKXXYZYTBA folk are moving to agree with the old Conservative position on the value of individual gun ownership. It will have a unifying effect in the United States and will ensure the eventual downfall of both the Republican and Democrat parties for having failed so miserably in their scripted prognoses of the American voter. With taxes being lower and the Federal Government making more revenue, Democrat-dependent myths about taxes are being exposed, but that doesn't indicate a nation moving toward a Republican establishment.

Cadence of Conflict: Asia, June 18

Trump has stopped military exercises near North Korea, but he has not initiated any plans to withdraw troops. His reason for stopping the exercises is that they are provocative and expensive. He has a point: If the heads of state are talking then we are less in need of fighting practice in a scenario where heads of state are not talking.

The military exercises with South Korea are expensive and provocative, as Trump explains. Frankly, they should stop. With healthy conversations and progress toward peace already behind us, there won't be a need for those drills any longer. Rehearsal for conflict that might never exist can often provoke the very conflicts we otherwise would not need to prepare for. As for the "expense" defense, few accountants will argue in favor of nickeling and diming away money as fiscally responsible and no one believes that taxpayers' pockets are infinitely deep except pundits with portfolios in public funding.

The Western news is that Trump is wrong, specifically with regard to China that China wins. According to this week's Western news narrative, China wins because of troop withdrawals that haven't happened, because a friend of China will de-nuke, and because over 30k US troops will be free to go home—or go to Taiwan, Mischief Reef, Vietnam, the Philippines, Japan, or any number of other Pacific island-nations China doesn't get along with.

Economically, China "wins" because manufacturing is leaving China—which must therefore mean that China's innovation and science is the new source of manufacturing elsewhere. Perhaps that includes innovation and science like the Chinese government now trying to track every car with a chip as of 2019. The "Mad Scientist" theorem of the experimental police state research moving from North Korea to China continues to play out.

Just remember with everything: There's more going on than anyone can see. Deals between governments are never fully explained to the public. They shouldn't be. But, as peace develops in one part of the western Pacific, hostilities move around and every pundit seizes opportunity to say, "I was right." No conflict is without news profiteering.

Encore of Revival: America, June 25

The world is shifting all over, not only in America. But, Americans are seeing the shift at home. It doesn't make headlines, but then again it is "trending", which makes headlines: Facebook is in peril. Zuckerberg overreached. While user privacy is one important topic, so is politically biased censorship.

It's legal to express one's political ideals, but it's also legal for Leftist-controlled companies to ban opposition views, citing "community" standards and guidelines as the excuse for censored speech. China does it and it's wrong in the Western mind, but what if Facebook and Twitter do it? Well, that's a different story, somehow.

Facebook and Twitter are publicly traded companies, thus regulated by the FTC. An argument could be made for publicly traded companies to be heavily fined—and the directors, executives, and operators fired—for censoring speech. But, this opens another debate. What about "hateful" religions that cultivate hate without actually crossing the line of "dangerous" hate speech?

The "giantness" of social media is a backlash against the "giant" media oldschool. But, social media giants are creating a backlash of their own.

FTC-regulated free speech isn't the solution to the implosion of social media giants. Instead, Facebook is doing a favor to its contenders. By being unfriendly, they are naturally encouraging their "customers" to shop elsewhere. This will have a far-reaching cascade effect and could make a swarm of new billionaires that eclipse Mark Zuckerberg, Elon Musk, and Jeff Bezos.

Cadence of Conflict: Asia, June 25

China is facing money problems, as the Western press continues to document in detail. China's economy is largely based on real estate. China's unusual form of communism includes laws that govern economics—especially with real estate, of course—and these laws are unusual in much of the rest of the world. As a result, people in China need to borrow money for things they normally wouldn't borrow money for. The repayment schedules are also strange.

The only way that a real estate business can stay afloat is if the prices of real estate keep rising. The more it rises, the more it needs to rise. Money doesn't fall from trees, but in China it needs to keep falling from somewhere in order to keep this vicious cycle spinning faster and faster. Eventually, the speed of the spinning wheel will exceed the strength of the wheel and it will all fly apart.

Then, we have China's strategy in the South Sea— also involving real estate. The man-made islands are complete. It all happened while the West watched closely and did nothing to stop it. They are heavily fortified and militarized.

Trump reminds the world that we aren't out of the woods yet with North Korea, Democrats misinterpret that as a contradiction—as if one step of progress means it's all over. Japan is ending its drills. The Korean problem is simmering down and Taiwan is escalating.

Now, we have the US strengthening its ties with Taiwan, the linchpin of the Pacific. Diplomats are visiting. Congressmen are calling for Taiwan's membership in sovereign-state-only organizations such as the UN. And, the Taiwan "Independence Party" welcomes US military cooperation.

Why would the US make such a bold move to side with Taiwan? Consider the US president's financial background: real estate. Trump understand's the economic crisis brewing in China. No one has said so, but the pieces line up. The US is positioning Taiwan as the main frontal push against China while the "attack from behind", as it were, is economics.

China is beefing up cyber attacks on Taiwan. US aircraft flying near the man-made islands are being hit by blinding flashes of light from the ground and from "fishing" boats, disrupting aviation. Using lasers such ways is illegal in war as both the US and China have signed agreements to.

China is also using drones that look like flying birds, but China wasn't the first. This technology has been used before. Interestingly, China has maintained a policy that tech manufactured in China must be shared with China's government. It would be even more interesting to see if any research surfaces on how many patent royalties China might owe for tech used to surveil its own people—surveillance only enabled by tech giants who caved into China's demands. But, due to the Tump administration, all that's coming to a grinding halt. If China wants better tech to spy on its own people, it's going to need to develop that tech on its own.

Those man-made islands in the South Sea were allowed to be built for a reason. Could they have been intended all along to become "booty" that will be "owned" by the West as Hong Kong was after the Opium Wars? Hong Kong just might be included if China is forced into concessions, especially with all the "ra-ra" fuss among spoiled Hong Kong students. The US strategy indicates many lofty "hopefuls" in the queue, should the status quo shift—in what direction no one knows. It seems that the Trump administration has aims much higher than merely settling disputes in Korea.

Encore of Revival: America, July 2

America is in great peril. A party is looking at winning the midterm right after winning the presidency. This is not normal and it doesn't matter how "wonderful" the party may seem at the time. Single-party rule is the death of the nation.

Mass shootings, Leftist protests, anger, rage, blame —the Left turns up the volume and the Republican party grows bigger.

The Republican Party is not what anyone thinks it is because the Republican Party isn't really a thing. This is the party that despised its own president, who is giving them this unusual midterm victory— but then suddenly gets behind him. This is not a party with normal values of conscience, but a party that gauges popular opinion and always arrives at the right conclusion too late—because that party actually has a moral compass quite different from the rest of the country.

Whatever that hidden moral compass is will only be seen after the party gains its supermajority and Trump leaves. From the moment he announced, Trump's biggest danger was always that he would succeed too well.

Give it ten years to ripen, but we live in the most dangerous time of the nation's history. Of course, there's always a chance to wake up and get it done right. But, the nation first needs to see the danger where it lies: in the hidden values of the always "failing" GOP, then to recognize that hope has already been kindled.

Cadence of Conflict: Asia, July 2

NBC reported news of recent months to counter news of recent weeks. It wouldn't be the first time NBC had a precarious definition of "news". Intelligence reports about very specific details of possible uranium production were broken as "news" by NBC. Bloomberg and others reported that NBC reported it. Taipei Times reported that Bloomberg reported that NBC reported it. NBC breaking this "older" news made more news than the outdated "news" itself. The whole claim smells smelly. It's likely a ruse, but we'll need about two weeks to know with confidence.

Hong Kongers like to protest so often that they are expected to protest annually. This year, protesters claimed a 50k head turnout; Hong Kong police estimated less than 10k, which would be a record low. Surely neither crowd estimate had any bias or motive to distort the numbers.

Remember, Hong Kong students like to protest more than is deserved. China could do better with counter-PR, but not much can be done when dealing with spoiled students. Don't be roused into hating China by the dwindling spoiled Hong Kongers. Protests are profitable in Hong Kong because they help sell newspapers in a market saturated with so many newspapers that they throw them at pedestrians on the sidewalks. Hong Kong's biggest problem is complacent Christians.

A more genuine problem of concern is the attention Chinese manufacturers are drawing from Western press coverage of Taiwan court rulings. Taiwan makes about 60% of the world's computer components. China wants in on the game and people are being prosecuted in Taiwan for stealing company secrets that would go to China. The biggest element of a case is in place: motive.

Most of the so-called "news" about trade wars are the most obvious. Companies are having problems with trade during a trade war. Really? This is considered news these days. Either that, or it is an obvious attempt to skirt the deeper issues behind the China-US trade war for global economy hopefuls hoping to sway public sentiment by reporting what was all foreseeable.

Encore of Revival: America, July 9

Facebook has been censoring many good things. Their procedures or automatic algorithms or whatever mechanism was designed to snag speech that just so happened to be from the Declaration of Independence was no isolated incident. Especially when a long train of abuses and usurpations evince a design, it's not coincidence, it's telling.

Facebook has had its hand caught in the cookie jar many times as of late. The social media giant doesn't seem interested in cultivating good will, but keeps working for excuses to drive away people who want to freely submit facts to a candid world via any platform but their own. Putting the post from The Vindicator newspaper back up won't prove to be enough. With trends and polls being what they are, the only way to prevent Facebook from taking a nosedive is for Zuckerberg to apologize for not endorsing Trump and write bots to flag posts praising Obama. That won't be fair, but it would be the only way to court favor lost among the bulk of its home-market customers who are subtly shopping elsewhere.

But, the biggest wire tripped by Facebook censoring the Declaration of Independence wasn't the people's irritation with Facebook, but the resulting alertness about the Declaration of

Independence. Facebook unwittingly helped make that document famous again. It seemed that America had forgotten all about it. Now, everyone is going to search and read what words created the safest nation in the world to hold such hot debates as the last two years, without fear of execution. For reclaiming attention to American history, Facebook has earned the first annual Pacific Daily Times Liberty of the Year award.

Thank you, Facebook, for reminding us of our heritage of freedom well fought for.

Cadence of Conflict: Asia, July 9

China is reaching out to the world. It doesn't want tariffs imposed by the US. President Xi Jinping likely feels betrayed by the man who was so kind to him previously, President of the United States Donald Trump. The Western press will of course paint China and Trump as the villains—each in their different sectors—while painting the consumer as the victim.

China's role is actually one of confusion. $500B one way and $100B another is fair if China is on the favorable end, of course. Why would someone be so cruel, using that as an excuse?

So, China is making its appeal to international bodies, such as the WTO. But, therein will befall another misunderstanding. The International community agrees on twelve nautical miles of ocean ownership, no more, and building islands doesn't count. China disagrees. So, appealing to International law won't work in China's favor, which will also seem unfair to the Chinese.

The Western press will make China out to be the bad guy, the aggressor. At the same time, the Western press will make Trump another bad guy for imposing tariffs. Of course China doesn't want tariffs, that much is understandable. But, coming to "China's" defense (actually their own) are the globalist businesses who believe that nationality, borders, and citizenship are a farce—that companies are the actual "nations" of the world. They are at war against both the US and China for not merging into one corporation. This is actually a battle for nationhood itself; from that perspective, both the US and China's responses make perfect sense.

As for China being the "bully" as portrayed by the Western press, China really doesn't see itself that way. The Chinese have no clue why the West would do such a thing, they really don't understand.

Encore of Revival: America, July 16

Trump is on tour, not without protesters who only know the version of America shown to them through less popular news outlets which, accordingly, need overseas audiences. Usually, good, working people stay home and at work, then vote in elections to change the landscape, while unpopular protesters demonstrate where it only makes non-binding noise. Still, it is good for all Britons to have their opportunity to voice their concerns, even to the leader of another nation.

Protesting and demonstrating are never bad. Once one tries to silence the opposition, such as the SJW movement in America has, tyranny's way is paved for those same silencers to be silenced on the pendulum's return.

Trump is neither kowtowing nor blaming in Europe, he is stating conflicts of interest. Take for example Germany's former president leading a company that will profit from Russia selling gas to Germany, while the US pays the bill to defend Germany from Russia. Something is terribly wrong there. Trump's repeat word for that seated pre-dinner speech was the word "inappropriate".

The Helsinki summit between Putin and Trump is overdue. Reagan made peace with his adversaries. Even Gorbachev took a long moment to pause the line while he reflected at the late president's visitation.

Diplomats behind desks in carpeted offices see negotiations as a way to greedily push for what they want, without concern for the other guy. As a business owner and negotiator, Trump understands that other countries want to help their economies grow and thrive. That will make a world of difference, likely to the world.

At home, the police in America only shoot and kill without a trial when it's the "bad guys". But, they seem to be exempt from US military rules of engagement: Do not fire until fired upon. The Chicago police video shows an officer with pistol in hand while revealing a pistol still in the suspect's belt. This is a difficult situation to judge.

Police want to keep people safe. Carrying a gun without proper training is dangerous, but the government doesn't offer the Constitutionally required militia training for all citizens. The Second Amendment gives that man a right to carry that gun just as he did, regardless of Chicago's unconstitutional laws. But, too many Blacks in America vote against the Constitution. Police should be softer in their approach, while their concerns about safety and desire to apprehend "bad guys" are still understandable.

It looks like SCOTUS's nominee Brett Kavanaugh will be approved by the Senate just as likely as any other. If by slim chance he isn't approved, the next nominee won't be any easier to pass through the

Senate. Whatever seat is up in the next round of a SCOTUS appointee will likely be more Conservative than Kavanaugh. But, the courts can sort out all of our problems. America really needs the same kind of sit-down that Putin is getting with Trump in Helsinki.

Cadence of Conflict: Asia, July 16

Global trade has become too congested and inbred. Enemies make vital weapons parts for each other— well, enemies of the US make vital weapons parts for the US, but don't return the favor. Western companies outsourced to developing markets, then were surprised at workplace hazards, loss in consumer trust, and didn't seem to anticipate that by sending jobs overseas they were downsizing their own customers.

The borderless fling wasn't going to last for a myriad of reasons—cultural incohesion being an impossibility for a manufacturing industry in denial, security conflicts of interest being a concern for Western powers. Internationalization is about governments and cultures understanding each other, not forcing cooperation between peoples who haven't yet learned to gel in the daily routines. Companies like Boeing got themselves too entangled in the scene of borderless manufacturing and are now whining and moaning because the inevitable finally happened. This indicates that their "globalist" action plan wasn't based in foresight, but delusional hopes.

Globalism is inevitable, but it won't take the path that the impatient hopefuls dreamed and thereby planned it would. Globalism needs cultural exchange to precede and exceed industrial integration, not vice versa. Boeing through the cart pulled its horse, banked on it, it backfired, and Boeing is now denying blame.

China and Europe, mainly Germany, are headed for the same blend of oil and water. This so-called "trade war" isn't setting well in China's market. Chinese people blame their government. That government doesn't want any misreporting that could even remotely influence the people into thinking that the unrelated trade and stock market could have any kind of direct relationship. The trouble Trump is making for China isn't demonstrated from rumors of censorship within China or its stock market, but in China's attempt for yet another foreseeably incohesive relationship with Germany. China is being smart, Germany is not.

China is owed everything by the West, but Germany hasn't figured this out yet. China doesn't need to say so because no one tells the obvious. A relationship between China and Germany would rightly favor China, Beijing would have no objection, but Berlin will cry and whine just as much as Boeing, once it all lays flat on the table. And, China will have made the profit.

Encore of Revival: America, July 23

The daily morning quest to prove, "Trump really stepped in it this time. Today, it's all over," has reached a point of certifiability. Recordings of Trump saying nothing wrong shouldn't even make news, let alone headlines. And, just the fact that Helsinki happened—not to mention that it won't be the last Putin-Trump summit—is good news, not bad. But, the anti-Trump press just doesn't see this.

The larger should-be piece of news with Helsinki would recall Trump's campaign statement that the US needed to get Edward Snowden back from Russia. But, Snowden didn't come up, spare a pre-summit article in the Politico. The most likely reason Snowden has fallen down on Trump's list of priorities is that Snowden blew the whistle on some sloppiness in the NSA. Trump's original statement against Snowden came about the same time Trump spoke in agreement with then FBI Director James Comey's desire to have Apple write a backdoor hack for their iPhones, another topic of technology that quietly disappeared. Whatever was going on in the Obama NSA and FBI has probably been fixed and bringing Snowden back into the limelight would show how sloppy inside baseball had gotten. It's probably best for everyone to just leave it alone.

If the press really wanted to injure Trump, they would have spun Snowden's situation as some kind of "failure", but they didn't. Instead, they are still stuck in their Russianewsgategate conspiracy kookery. By pushing as far as they did this past week, they are truly making themselves irrelevant. This week crossed a new line of crazy for the press.

The most important development this week was not that the queen appointed Charles her successor nor that the new American president met with Russia's president for the first time nor that Hillary gave a sit-down talk in a moo-moo, but that the press is going insane in public view and doesn't care. This could shift the balance in the mass media market. Watch for trending changes around the start of August 2018.

Cadence of Conflict: Asia, July 23

Central planning has only so much room for slight of hand tricks to keep up its sleeve. When the going gets tough, everyone goes home. For China, that means devaluing its currency, a complaint Trump has long lobbed against the trade giant.

Maintaining good relations with Apple and almost achieving the manufacturing capability long held by Samsung is quite the accomplishment for the Chinese. Good job. Everyone owes them a hand. China's BOE company hopes to be able to start manufacturing the flexible, "organic" LED displays by 2020.

Devaluing currency as a response to trade tariffs from the US, however, is likely to make those tariffs higher, considering that devaluation of its own currency was one reason Trump argued for tariffs before his election. This, and turning to Africa, means that the international bite is felt. Silicon Valley also has its eyes on Africa, meaning that Apple and China may meet again in Africa, as well as Google. But, doing more of the same things that initiated tariffs is likely to cause more tariffs than tariff problems it alleviates.

China has a hard set of choices ahead and as those choices narrow, the tiger will feel more and more like its been backed against a corner. This path doesn't endure entirely peacefully.

Encore of Revival: America, July 30

Days after Trump meets with Putin and doesn't mention Snowden, the NSA finds "many issues of non-compliance" in handling data, which was part of Snowden's initial concern. It seems that a way may already be finding its way for Snowden to return to the US in relative peace.

Just after the worldwide worry machine was all in a tizzy about trade wars with the EU, the US and EU have almost all their issues resolved and are working to make things much better than they were before.

The "bug" in Putin's soccer ball is part of an app device from Adidas, not a surveillance device from Russia's FSB.

The "made in China" Trump products either 1. go back to the pre-presidential campaign Trump business in which Trump learned about China up close and personal as a trader himself or 2. are unaffiliated knock-off products made in China to resemble actual Trump campaign products, but Bernie Sanders doesn't know the difference between the real and the knock-off.

Now, the Leftist press is going after SCOTUS nominee Kavanaugh's wife. There is a gross hypocrisy here since the Leftist press didn't go digging through the correspondence of Clinton's mistresses. When Congress did hold an inquiry about Bill's love life through Independent Counsel Kenneth Starr, the Leftist press jumped to write it off as "personal". It doesn't seem personal anymore, or is it getting too personal?

The reason for going after Kavanaugh's wife is lack of evidence against Kavanaugh. This goes beyond "grasping at straws". The implosion of the press reached a new public demonstration of insanity this week, so the weeks to come are only likely to get more entertaining.

Cadence of Conflict: Asia, July 30

The "China miracle" was nothing more than smoke and mirrors as big companies of the West took advantage of Chinese people seeking a living and Western consumers seeking lower prices. Everyone lost. There was no "miracle".

The fad for cutting costs and quick investment returns nickeled and dimed away quality, eventually pushing bean counters to fall in love with China's underpaid labor force. When China opened for business in 1978, the shipments rolled in. Wealth wasn't made, it was only rearranged. A large shipping freighter made a large wake, some sunbathers had to move their towels on the beach when the wave wrecked the sand castles, and the global economist footsie-frat claimed that the sea levels had permanently risen.

Perhaps the label was wishful thinking, perhaps it was a malicious deception, but it wasn't Chinese propaganda; it was globalist propaganda. China's "growing economy" was fueled by an exchange between a planned economy and the free markets of the world. Whatever wave came, it would lower, eventually balance out, and could never have endured any more than spilled crude oil mixes with wildlife on the beach.

The mainstream Western press kept reporting on the "Chinese miracle", encouraging Beijing that China's new economy was here to stay. Western globalist economists should have known better, maybe they did, maybe they didn't, but China is paying the price of the inevitable. Eventually, either the Western economies would collapse—then the one-way flow of cash into China would stop as it did after the opium wars—or a Donald Trump would come along and stop the flow before it got that far. But, it wasn't going to last. The biggest victim of the bean-counter coupon-clipper culture of the West is China. And, making victims reaps nothing more than ill will.

Encore of Revival: America, August 6

It's fair to guess by now, as a kid, Trump might have learned to tell "white lies" to cover up things that might be personally embarrassing. Such is a high-energy culture in many parts and classes of the world. Energetic people from all walks of life might not even remember what they had for breakfast and instinctively say, "I did not pick my nose," when caught picking their noses on camera. And, so what!?

That's the relevant question: So what? So what if Donnie was caught picking his nose? So what if he lies in denying it? Good people don't care about picking noses or lying about picking noses; those who do care are petty. Stupid accusations get stupid defenses. This is how the public will respond to the purported "admission" that some meeting with Russians was about Hillary. It wasn't about illegally rigging vote count, which is more than can be said for some precincts, which Mueller is not investigating.

The latest news feeds from every morning always have the Leftist media hopeful that "this will be the news break that brings down Trump"—and it never does. The AP story this time even has a picture of Trump waving at a Morristown, NJ airport as if it's "goodbye". It's not goodbye at all.

The media and Left think that Americans listen to news to be told what to think. So, when Conservatives listen and read about opinions to inspire their own ideas, the Leftist media presumes that they are minions being told what to think and do. But, the majority of Americans are not minions being told what to think. And, the Christians didn't become Christians by letting the Leftist media try to tell them what to think nor will Christians take orders from the Leftist media on where lies fit within Christian morals—morals which the Leftist media hates anyway. And, they certainly won't decide to unelect Trump just because he might be a "white liar" who covers up embarrassing blunders that they don't care about anyway.

Left-leaning voters already have their minds made up. So, the bombardment of the Leftist media tolling Trump has no hope of removing Trump from office, but only to throw the ordinary American who votes Democratic into a frenzy. The best thing is to just ignore the gossip and stop caring about what everyone says about what Donnie says he did or didn't do.

But danit, everyone should learn from the Christians: Truth sets us free. Hit back with the bold truth and watch the truth do the rest for you.

Cadence of Conflict: Asia, August 6

Apple sales are up in China, which creates a problem on two fronts. First, the doomsayers were wrong about tariffs crashing economies. If the tariffs aren't making a difference according to the globalist economists, then why did they object? They're the "experts", after all. Shouldn't they have foreseen that tariffs wouldn't matter? The second problematic front is that an American company's success seems to be a problem for the Chinese.

Apple doesn't filter and censor content from personal users, but Chinese state-media outlets seem to think it should. Even though Apple proved that China is good for business, someone had to find fault. Good news just won't do these days.

So, now it's Apple vs China rather than Apple in China. It seems Apple was also duped by the globalist economists into vesting one fifth of its sales in a relationship that wasn't going to last. Watch. This looks like a preemptive step to take action against Apple, who would do well to start pulling out of China before its assets get appropriated for the benefit of the Chinese people.

The swelling trade war between the US and China isn't going away. Dating back to the Opium Wars, the West will push and push as long as most of the money flows downhill into China. While China compares tariffs, Trump balances cash flow.

More importantly, China could be entering another "danger zone" of its own. Painting Trump as an enemy in China's own newspapers could inspire dissidents within China that they have support from the US. The best response for China's own stability would be to report that Trump's tariffs were intended to help China's economy more than the US. That would be more likely to promote unity among the Chinese people. But, the state didn't think of that before press time and the newspapers can't be recalled, even when owned by the state.

China is, indeed calm, just as it claims. There should be no question that China believes the flow of money into China is fair. Chinese don't want to be unfair, after all. China should only have favorable trade because China deserves it. Beigjing isn't out to hurt anyone, unless they are denied the extra favor that the world owes to China. So, don't let the Western press convince you that China is more of a monster than it actually is. We can all be monsters at times.

Encore of Revival: America, August 13

What happened to Omarosa is normal, it doesn't matter, and it's a darn shame that it's normal and doesn't matter. Bureaucratic America permeates every institution, from universities to small Christian congregations to telecommunications companies, even to the White House. They run people around, play dirty tricks, mistreat people of all skin tones, and now it's coming back to bite them in the hiney.

Omarosa herself is now under the microscope, which lets us see the shameful sham of why her story doesn't matter. It's just too normal. Bureaucracy doesn't attack everyone, but it sure does have its favorites. She seems to be one of them. Chuck Todd kept asking how and why she knew to record her meeting with White House Chief of Staff John Kelly. It's unbelievable for most people, except for bureaucracy's favorite people to bash. After a while bureaucracy victims get a nose for smelling the rigmarole around the corner. And, they have a knack for attracting trouble, if for no other reason than that bureaucracy doesn't like bloodhounds sniffing them down.

Here's how the archetypal scenario could likely play out—not how it actually did, but how it could have if bureaucracy behaves like bureaucracy...

Trump knows that worms in the White House are always trying to control him by controlling the information that gets to him. So, he asks Omarosa to get certain articles for him, going around his bureaucracy. Smelling trouble, she may have taken steps to protect herself, just as she did in recording the conversation, just as she did with giving her loves ones copies of the reported recording of Trump using the "N" word as a precaution just "in case she's rubbed out" (Esquire). That kind of preemptive-precautionary habit might have led her to violate some rules in the White House, though she would have been acting in defense, not hostility. John Kelly, like the classic bureaucrat he comes across as in the recording, wouldn't have been out of character to "trump" up, as it were, his firing case against Omarosa, though he wouldn't have been entirely unjustified either. She was likely a loose canon, which was why Trump wanted her there in the first place, and John Kelly arrived to tie down loose canons. Trump later told her that he "delegated" because he really did delegate. Trump wouldn't fire the lady himself since he adores her too much—this happens with many administrators because no one likes to fire friends. And, no one likes it when your good friend, the President, lets his chief fire you because you got too cautious on someone else's watch. Feelings are hurt, it wasn't meant to be personal, but it was personal. Now, hell hath no fury like a woman scorned.

...That's an archetypal speculation of how things may have gone down the hill.

Trump kept things chaotic on purpose so that an old boys' club couldn't keep him a prisoner of fame. This was the story on the street when Reince Priebus left. The Left praised John Kelly as the one possible man who might be able to control Trump. When he was first hired, Kelly was hailed by the Left as the savior. Now, when he does what the Left praised him for, it's all Trump's fault.

The words Kelly spoke were shamefully typical and ordinary in bureaucratic America, but they don't make him especially evil. Many, many pastors have been "fretired" through the same conversation in the back office. Coming from the White House raises the stakes, but other than that, the conversation seemed all too typical.

As for the "N" word, one statement doesn't define a person. It can be sad. But, everyone has said foolish things that they didn't mean, whether in stupidity or anger. No president will ever be an exception. In the minds of Trumpists, who only grow their numbers, discovering proof that a human is human is no longer a fireable offense.

Omarosa was a way for Trump to get around his own gatekeeper. If Trump doesn't hire Omarosa back, Kelly could end up "resigning" in the coming months.

The wisest action would be for Trump to have a one-on-one with Omarosa, apologize on a personal level for his own bureaucracy—which every institution in America has, shamefully—, hire her back so that only he has the power to fire her, also keep Kelly on to keep doing his job, and encourage her that she won't need to guard herself with more recordings and possible "ethics" violations anymore.

And, if he did use the "N" word, he should also say to the country, "Yeah, I did. I was an idiot, really sorry to everyone. Don't follow my bad example. Let's all be better and move one."

Cadence of Conflict: Asia, August 13

China's situation isn't getting easier. Taiwan now has tested a new missile, boasting ability to fire within China's mainland, being capable of destroying military targets on both land and sea. This is no laughing matter. On the economic front, Beijing has a hard-headed counterpart in the White House, Donald Trump. He shows no indication of backing down on any front, including Beijing. Now, China is going after Muslims.

While it can be politically incorrect for the West to pursue terrorists if they are Muslim, China doesn't have that problem. Military states rarely do, which is one advantage China has over the West. Terror cells may be in hot water since China is on high alert in all directions. If Taiwan were to create trouble on its eastern coast, Beijing would not want more trouble from its western borders. So, any earlier preemptive action from Beijing is likely to be westward, toward Muslim nations. Those Muslim areas could be in greater danger than Taiwan.

Taiwanese have been busy, though. When anyone uses the "Taiwan, China" format, Taiwanese go berserk. That's raising a lot of attention about a little island in the Pacific which now has missiles capable of attacking China. These are interesting times.

Encore of Revival: America, August 20

John Brennan, the former CIA director, was part of the Obama administration. His views are part and parcel of pro-Obama, anti-Trump groupthink. What does a former CIA director need a security clearance for anyway? He's not directing anymore—at least he shouldn't be. Though he accuses the sitting president of treason, he has his own security issues, questions of treason being among them. His opinion is anything but objective, impeccable, or unbiased.

The supposed impeccable Robert Mueller's investigation is going nowhere. It was going nowhere at warp speed, but now is slowing to a snail's race. The New York Times is going over the top with one of its greatest "BS" articles ever. The recent and controversial article on Don McGahn doesn't have much substance, though the style is that of breaking news.

Giuliani is right, there is an attempt to make Trump enter a perjury trap under the guise of testifying. That would be the only purpose of Trump testifying under the groupthink sentiment Brennan became the face of this week. The anti-Trump groupthink already sees Trump as guilty, not of treason, but for not being pro-Obama. To them, the sentence ought to be greater than that of treason. By speaking out and seeking to maintain his security clearance even though he is no longer director, Brennan is demonstrating how far the Russianewsgategate scandal network weaves.

Most of what developed this week was marketing. Brennan's public statements put him in the perfect position to launch a book, already having dramatized himself as the new champion of his groupthinkalikes. If he announces a book, it could have a success overnight. Then, we have the BS article in the New York Times. At last, we have the most incredible claim ever made by Russian hack conspiracy kooks: that they will believe whatever is true based only on what Trump says in a perjury trap because they haven't yet made up their minds. Yeah, right.

Cadence of Conflict: Asia, August 20

The silent war between the Koreas is shifting to family reunions. Families split by the war are having a get-together today in the North. Trump has a deal with Kim Jong Un. Peace is moving forward, and Korean reunification along with it. Reunification is one of China's values and things look great as they are. So, why does Xi Jinping need to go to North Korea? Does he also have family there? Perhaps he's trying to market himself.

China has been busy marketing itself around the world as of late, as has Taiwan. So goes the other silent war—the silent war between China and Taiwan, though it's becoming not quite so silent. Taiwan's President Tsai Ingwen traveled this week. While in California, she did one of the most controversial and disrespectful things a president could do: She visited a coffee shop. Oh, China is so angry! How dare she do that!

The Taiwanese coffee chain, 85°C, has a few locations in California and Tsai Ingwen went to one of them. They even gave her a bag. She did that just to spite China! That's all she ever thinks about. It's not that great of a coffee shop anyway. Don't visit there and try any of their lattes or cappuccinos or any of their many desserts. There are better things to do than just trying to spite China.

China protested, of course, as they rightly should for such a disrespectful thing Tsai Ingwen has done. Taiwan's Premier, William Lai, lashed back, as did Tsai Ingwen. They think China's not marketing itself rightly by objecting to evil things like visiting coffee shops. They want China to have a good image, but right now they think China's doing it the wrong way. What the heck do they know anyway?

Taiwan has its own marketing problems. Former AIT director, the envoy from America to Taiwan, William Stanton says that Taiwan needs to market itself better. While things cool off in the Koreas, the marketing battle between the China's is just warming up.

Encore of Revival: America, August 27

Senator John McCain is dead, God rest his soul. So are three gamers in their 20s, killed by suicide gamer rage at a computer competition in Florida.

Trump was busy golfing on Sunday and only Tweeted about a media spin article, explaining how Obama was receiving credit for economics that developed under Trump policy. Ivanka Tweeted thoughts and prayers to the victims at the gamer event shooting in Jacksonville, Florida. The Left didn't like that because not grandstanding for seizure of guns means doing nothing. Trump is in a catch-22.

From the "Fake Right", Alex Jones and Oliver Stone continue to entertain Conservatives of the hyperactive, hermit niche, who feed on fear. Stone predicts that Don Jr. will be indited. We'll see. Both taking heads of the now-dubbed "Stone & Jones" show (courtesy PD Times) shriek about how the other got harassed, but not injured permanently because the show continues. If the Leftist rent-a-mobs ever stop gaggling Stone & Jones, their show could be over. Then what will keep us entertained?

The Mueller investigation seems to be going in such a doomed and distracted multi-direction that it could be re-labeled the "Mueller investigation", but for different reasons. So, at least the show will continue somewhere. The real question will be whether "Stone & Jones" show viewers hold Stone accountable to make accurate predictions. If he's right, they should be bored. If he's right and they are hysteric, it means they are fanatic. If he's wrong, and they don't drop viewership, they are either fanatic or bored.

We're all led to believe that Trump doesn't know exactly what he's doing. But, his image of incompetence must hold up if he is ever to endure through the battle of wits looming in the Pacific, particularly the Northwest Pacific.

Cadence of Conflict: Asia, August 27

The Pacific is heating up bigtime. Just after Kim Jong Un meets with Chinese President Xi Jinping, Trump calls off a cabinet member's visit to Pyongyang the day after the new North Korean envoy was announced. What was that all about? Consider China.

China has been moving in on Taiwan aggressively, both through marketing and through international relations. The TOEFL test given in Taiwan lists Taiwan as a province of China, using the controversial, "Taiwan, China" nomenclature. Taiwanese were furious because the US government requires tests such as the TOEFL, which is administered by ETS, a nonprofit organization based in New Jersey. How does a US government recognized US-based English testing organization come to list a testing market contrary to how the US State Department does? The answer is: pressure from China.

Companies around the world have been strong-armed by China into listing Taiwan as a province of China. In the past weeks and months, airlines were required to comply in order to continue flying to China, many waiting until the last possible moment. This week, a PhD candidate at the University of Salamanca in Spain Tweeted a letter from China last October essentially demanding that the university shut down "Taiwan Cultural Days".

Now, Taiwan ended ties with El Salvador for recognizing China instead of Taiwan. This came after Taiwan declined for a year to make a sizable investment in the Port of La Union. Taiwan was concerned about debt for both countries. Senator Marco Rubio wasn't happy and a bill has already been amended to cut US funding to El Salvador.

While North Korea doesn't seem to be making as big of strides as expected in denuclearization, China is cozying up to North Korea while soon-to-be-former US allies cozy up to China and while China and Taiwan exchange lobbing spit wads. The overall situation doesn't look good for the pro-US side. But, there's always more than meets the eye.

Encore of Revival: America, September 3

It's all seen in his funeral. John McCain's death, more and more, seems destined to symbolize the death of the Washington "establishment". Put less friendlily, the death of McCain was the death of the swamp. More respectfully, and how things out to be, we mourn the loss of a senator while we move on with our convictions.

The Trump electorate, finally gaining the cooperation of the GOP, is proving more and more to be a valid and clear and enduring majority. They wanted Obama's health care law repealed; only McCain—from their own political party—stopped them. They wanted to be descent and quiet at the funeral of the man who despised them. John McCain found Sarah Palin, then put her on a leash. She respected him and only spoke respectfully of him, then he put a muzzle on her. Now, he's dead and she continues to respect him in her silence. Meghan McCain had a right to say whatever she wanted and her words agreed with her father's sentiment; Trumpists didn't like her words, but she stayed right on topic. Thank you Meghan. Trump would not attend, but his daughter did, a most appropriate discretion. Trump had more respect in his absence than in Obama's venomous distraction toward the man who would not crash a funeral. Bush and Biden gave good and respectful speeches, celebrating and mourning him.

The Trump electorate lives on and they are growing in number. Now, with Kevin McCarthy calling an inquisition into the Silicon Valley tech giants, who have harassed the controlling votership for two years, Republicans are moving away from the maverick-moderate tactics of McCain—which did work in his day. Insulting and muffling public expression, including the Declaration of Independence, was a foolish error. If their defense is true—that they "didn't know"—then they should have at least studied the electorate rather than despised it and known their own history well enough not to flag key words from our nation's heritage. At least, Silicon Valley is guilty of not caring enough about what they should. They are already paying a punishment through the markets. Now, they will answer to Congress.

McCarthy's move will energize the base—the one thing that the losing moderates of 2014 feared— the one thing that helps Republicans win elections. The Republican base is energized and we are now no longer looking at a possible and unusual midterm victory for Republicans; we are now looking at a likely and unusual midterm victory for Republicans.

Cadence of Conflict: Asia, September 3

China is in trouble. We don't know why, but we know the indication: Trump will be absent from ASEAN. He was absent from a funeral this week and his support grew. He was absent from a Republican debate, then he won the Republican nomination. By not meeting Xi face to face, Xi won't be able to read his emotions. No one knows exactly what Trump has planned, only that he's spending a lot of time on the golf course—a luxury banned by China's Communist Party—a luxury that just so happens to be Trump's favorite place to mull things over and get new ideas.

In the rainy season of August, Taiwan enjoyed almost three weeks of cloud cover. Whatever went on in Taiwan, it was difficult to see from above, and China never likes not being able to see from above. There's nothing like a little conveniently bad weather to irritate the away team. But, that wasn't the end.

The US is looking at a contingency of Marines to defend its unofficial embassy in Taipei and a former chief suggests simulating attacks on China's Soviet made, diesel powered aircraft carrier, the Liaoning, if it gets close enough to Taiwan. Such a statement is purely provocative and no chief, former or sitting, would make such provocation without sitting in counsel. This all compares to the Scottish flashing each other before a battle of the kilts. This week, the Taipei Times published numerous insulting and blatantly disrespectful stories from Taiwanese politics, spitting at China. Taiwan wouldn't do without backing.

Encore of Revival: America, September 10

Assuming Jeff Sessions does not recuse himself again, if and when he investigates the mole undermining the will of the people now elected to the White House, he should look for someone akin to a spotless East Coast grad with a sense of personal duty, a history of "high grad" military status over real life, reverence for sailors like John McCain, little time in life to have acquired entrepreneurial startup bearings, and knowing how to correctly use the word "lodestar" along with a proper em dash—. In other words, they should look for someone similar to John Kelly.

As for the economy, it's the economy stupid. Republicans should win the midterm. Everything else is just excitement about excitement. Blue collar union workers usually vote blue, but don't count on it with them getting higher pay. As if that wasn't enough, this little maritime-savvy maverick hero from the White House just might bring out the vote enough to boost the republican electorate participation. Then, we also have all those #walkaway peeps, who are snowballing against the snowflakes.

The biggest mistake in Woodward's book was spelling Trump's name correctly. All press is good press, especially when the economy is clipping along.

As for Elon Musk's fall in stock prices, that sure does fit with his goal of making the company private again. If prices fall below his promised $420/share, his offer would seem attractive.

Cadence of Conflict: Asia, September 10

Right or wrong, the US-China tariff war was always coming. Stupid American companies flew into the campfire of Chinese manufacturing like moths into a flame. China was smart inasmuch as they did not become dependent on the outsourced labor, which was always going to ever-only be temporary. China has wasted no time, building infrastructure, such as the highway between Hong Kong and Macau and the silk road, now gaining income by the well marketed tourist attraction.

But, this tariff war was always coming. The political situation in the Pacific indicates that it's not about economics so much as it is about military. Pacific island nations grow more and more irritated by China. Little, small nations are speaking out, demanding China apologize for storming out of a PIF (Pacific Islands Forum) meeting when China's diplomatic representative was told to wait to speak until after heads of state from member nations had their turn. China is not a member, only an attendee. This is not any demonstration of leadership that the region will accept, no matter how much it may have been bestowed by the territorial gods at the universe's center, which is in China of course.

Then, there's Taiwan. If last week was a week of firing off blanks and papers across bows, this week, cannonballs started splashing. Taiwan introduced three different bills amending existing law, stiffening restrictions and penalties concerning anything that could even remotely be construed as interference between Taiwan and China. As if that wasn't enough, Taiwan is increasing its budget for both fighter jets and the navy. And, Taiwan's military even moved up an annual naval exercise to rehearse an attack from China at an earlier date than usual.

In all of this, the rain continues to fall in Taiwan, now flooding different parts of the island than saw torrents over three solid weeks of cloud cover. Not to worry, though. City governments are closely monitoring just how many millimeters of water can drain away how quickly, revamping any old sewer system that can't keep up. Taiwan just seems to have its hands full, as well as its rivers.

Then, there is the tsunami of US diplomacy. Trade wars often prelude military wars. While Taiwan's dwindling allies flip to support China, the US is breaking ties with any country that breaks ties with Taiwan, more or less. Solidarity with Taiwan seems to have bipartisan support in US Congress. With trade alliances shifting, when war breaks out, it will be a financial calculation as a convergence of China's revenue and US dependence on Chinese-made goods both bottom out.

Encore of Revival: America, September 17

Trump's sanctions about elections are about the election. Turn all eyes to Texas. The seat of Senator Ted Cruz should not be in jeopardy. Democrats have no reason to dump such large amounts of money into a Texas race where senators are trending Republican—unless they are either crazy or they happen to know about other plans that could affect the vote. They aren't campaigning against Cruz because they think he is weak, but because he is so powerful.

Without the additional sanctions on foreign interference, it would be much easier to meddle in your opponent's election by asking a foreign power to do the meddling. Americans know better than to meddle in American elections because they have nowhere to run. Off-shore meddlers are another story—at least they were until Trump ordered his sanctions.

This is a shot across the bow, not so much deterring foreign powers from meddling as much as making foreign powers—and any domestic cooperatives—aware that the White House is aware that there are attempts to meddle. Only a fool would think Trump's order is purely for the optics of pleasing his unusually loyal base, which cares more about jobs and walls than defusing accusations they have already decided are fraudulent. These sanctions from the White House could be what wins Cruz his second term. We'll see.

US Ambassador to the United Nations Nikki Haley lives in a unit in the famed Waldorf Astoria. She originally had the $135k/month unit occupied by Susan Rice during the Obama years. Rice had ordered $52k worth of drapes and motors to close them, but the furnishings didn't arrive until Haley had insisted on moving to a less-than-half-the-price unit of the lavish Obama ambassador, at only $58k/month. New York is an expensive place for everyone, but Haley also rejected the set of drapes. Of course, in New York newswriting, Obama's bad decision must be blamed on Trump. It's all Trump's fault what Obama did.

Senator Feinstein should be impeached and Judge Kavanaugh should be approved Monday rather than Thursday. After a long and—according to Democrats—interesting career in the White House, an uncorroborated claim from a supposed victim of a so-called assault—much less severe than anything Clinton was praised for by his base—came to Feinstein in July. The accuser didn't mention anything in all the other years of Kavanaugh's career, nor did Feinstein mention the accusations in July or August. Everyone waited until the last possible minute.

If it is true that Democrats don't mention important facts until time is almost up, they should be expelled from Washington. Many voters in the #WalkAway movement seem to agree. But, this looks more like something made-up. By doing this at such a late hour, Democrats have implied that there is nothing more meaningful to discuss. Democrats are still angry that they can't read all the private memorandum that other people wrote to other people which Kavanaugh was the confidential delivery boy for. So, they pull an Anita Hill style accusation that looks fake in every time and manner they choose. The only credibility this accuser can gain at the bottom of this ninth inning would be for Feinstein to resign in disgrace for either trying to pull a fake "September surprise" or for exploiting a victim in doing so. Fat chance on a Democrat not exploiting the victims so desperately engineered into their voter base.

Cadence of Conflict: Asia, September 17

The US is not sending a contingency of Marines to Taiwan to protect it's envoy. This announcement came after reports that the US had such plans. After discussing the non-existence of the plans for deployment, the State Department also discussed that it does not discuss plans for security or other strategies. Perhaps the real strategy not being discussed is that the strategy is not being discussed.

At any rate, the announcement that an announcement has not been made about the discussion of not discussing security strategy and the non-discussion about Marines who will not be deployed should make heads in Beijing spin as they try to figure out just what the US is not doing about what it's not discussing. Fewer Marines in Taiwan would be more inviting for an invasion, if the discussion were under discussion, which it is not—reportedly.

One of the best kept secrets about the brewing trade war between the US and China is that US jobs departed to China. A trade war would move those jobs back to the US.

Consider a US company that set up shop in China. While the financial know-it-alls loose sleep over anything being less pleasant than an afternoon massage, including a US company in China being attacked hyena style as Chinese culture loves to do, the people in the US wouldn't care about that company. That's the company that forsook the American worker. In the mind of the average US working voter, the company that got in bed with China should stay around for the abusive marriage; so leave them to the hyenas! Any Americans who own shares in those companies would do well to keep that information secret from their working, voting neighbors.

The world doesn't work how so-called "financial experts" think it does. The trade war will not hurt the US economy because economies flourish from jobs, not consumption. Claiming that lower consumption of off-shore goods will harm a market would be to measure a farm's profitability based on how much the farming family eats other farmers' food. The real issue with the trade war is a real war.

Encore of Revival: America, September 24

Things are looking bad for social media giants and for Democrats. Senator Feinstein really stuck her foot in it this time. Now, she questions the truthfulness of her own token "me too" witness. Questioning herself won't help her credibility when she sat on an accusation for two months.

Social media outreached as well. But, that's to be expected when a CEO is so wet behind the ears that the only leadership he remembers from his years of actually paying attention to politics were filled with Obama-topia. Zuckerberg hasn't lived long enough to have ever seen what went around actually come back around. Maybe Trump's response to his shenanigans will help him develop an attention span and it might lead to his own "red pill" moment, should he join #WalkAway himself, but let's not get too far ahead of ourselves.

The bigger focus should be on Trump's strategy. For the first time since Reagan, as an election approaches, someone is actually acting more like a Republican. The Republicans would do well to follow Trump's lead. Republican voters only wake up and go vote when candidates act like Republicans, not political pansies. Two moderate, wishy-washy, failed Obama opponents proved that well enough. Expect more Republican activity from Republicans.

Times are changing. The #WalkAway movement is only growing. Now, dissing Democrats has become the way to get YouTube likes from Obama voters. If you make promises, you'd better deliver on them. That's what Trump is doing, anyway. And, his numbers don't seem so low.

Cadence of Conflict: Asia, September 24

Google has gone off the deep end. The level of insanity matches The Bridge over the River Kwai. Actually helping China spy—Are Google execs loopy? From a Chinese company inside China that would make sense. But, Google is American. As if helping a non-ally spy isn't enough, social media giants are already in trouble over censorship in the US. Google could be in bigger trouble with the White House than Wall Street is.

Taiwan hasn't wasted any time irritating China. Now, a temple that was bought seven years ago by a Taiwanese business man, which was then converted into a "shrine to Chinese communism", is having the lights and water turned off as the local government prepares to demolish the whole place. That won't wash over well for anyone hoping to court friendship with China.

China seems to be taking the hint and finally getting offended. Beijing cancelled a trip to talk trade with Washington after figuring out that tariffs were set by imbalance and retaliation rather than rhetoric. As for the two steering factors— imbalance and retaliation—China shows no indication of making concessions. But, it's not the tariffs or trade talks that deserve the headlines as much as the insults mounting against China.

The US is going after Russia for selling weapons to China. That's even more irritation. And, China is even more angry. If we were to analyze the events of the past few months, even years more subtly, it could seem that angering China was an accident. But, the recent past makes more sense, just as events are more easily anticipated, if we consider that the US is irritating China on purpose. Expect more insults from the US, along with Taiwan.

And, Korea. Yes, the two nations are getting along. That won't work well for any nation or pundit hoping to argue that Trump doesn't know how to make a difference in the region.

Encore of Revival: America, October 1

In the words of Tyrion Lannister, "Making honest feelings do dishonest work is one of her many gifts." Something is very wrong about the testimony against SCOTUS nominee Judge Kavanaugh. But, that doesn't matter. The odd smiles and giggles from both the witness and her attorney, the "crying" voice without shedding one single tear, many frequent flights from someone afraid to fly when it came time to testify in a matter she wanted investigated, refusing to be interviewed in her home state while demanding an investigation, heavy use of "attorney-client privilege" from an accuser who could prove her case better by not exercising that privilege on key questions whose answers could support her case, a lie detector test administered between flights after a funeral paid for by no one knows who—none of that matters.

For the attorney blocking a question about whether Dr. Ford was informed that she could be questioned per her request, in her own state, he should be subpoenaed or Dr. Ford, her attorney, and her allegations should be dismissed—since Democrats think unusually high standards are so vital. Even Republican Senator Lindsey "Gramnesty", who voted for Obama's justices, adamantly defends Kavanaugh, arguing that, as a former judge himself, not so much as a warrant could be issued with such little information Dr. Ford provided at this suspiciously and conveniently late hour.

When Kavanaugh admitted to drinking in high school, he lowered his odds of Republican favor more than any accusation could. If that doesn't take his name out, nothing will. Democrats don't oppose him because they have a shred of belief in the witness against him, but because they know he would vote as a supreme court justice in agreement with the Declaration of Independence—that life is an unalienable human right—because they don't want any judge who upholds the nation's founding documents. If Democrats wanted credibility for their emotional appeal in grandstanding, they would vow before the nation to approve the next pro-Life judge appointed before the November election. But, that is just what they hope to prevent.

Even if true, these accusations shouldn't matter. The "boys will be boys" defense is false and no one credible is making that argument, though Democrats rebut the wind. Kavanaugh has become a better person and done good and honest things since high school, so it seems anyway. He knows how to grow up. Bill Clinton doesn't. That's what matters. But, none of what matters seems to matter to Democrats. Where was Senator Feinstein during the Clinton years?

There could be some shred of truth to the allegations, but the manner and circumstances in which it has been presented has many predictable and craftable conveniences that just so happen to line up with Democrat party politics. If one single Democratic senator cared about these harassment charges, that senator would have voted to impeach Clinton. By Democrat standards—politician and voter alike—Kavanaugh almost qualifies as enough of a "bad boy" for the presidency.

Regardless of the senate committee's decision, Republican voters will be furious. This could trigger a cascade turnout in November that tips the Republican favor even more than speculated thus far.

Cadence of Conflict: Asia, October 1

When China cancelled a meeting in Washington, the Chinese thought they were sending a message; Washington thought they wouldn't be sending any more messages at all. The Chinese government wants mutual respect, trade that results in equal numbers, and that countries not be bullied into taking sides in a China-US disagreement. Though China lobbed this new policy in a complaint against the US, there have yet to be steps or specific commitments on how China will hold up its side of this new policy. It will be difficult to get clarification without communication.

US tariffs are unfair. It's so obvious that it doesn't need to be proven. China has a right, after all—and everyone should agree—to develop itself as a nation. China's right to have any and all resources given to it from everywhere in the world, to whatever extent is needed for development, is an entitlement China has by birth and is already universally accepted around the world. Those in the US who oppose this obvious consensus are a rogue fringe not deserving of academic mention.

But, Taiwan is being a big bully—a meanie-face. By not rebuking the US for considering a third of a billion dollar arms sale to Taiwan, the Taiwanese are spitting in Beijing's face once again. As if that bullying wasn't enough, Taiwan is also planning a new place to park its helicopters. Of all the audacity!

Hong Kong, however, stands no chance against the great and mighty China. By banning a pro-independence party, the Hong Kong government sure showed them! There's no possible hope for any kind of backlash or rise in sympathy, once the rightful leaders have made their all-powerful will known in the fully self-governed special administrative region of Hong Kong.

Encore of Revival: America, October 8

The confirmation of Brett Kavanaugh opens a new problem for Conservatives: supermajority. Any unchecked party is dangerous. Breyer and Ginsberg are aging. If one of them resigns or passes within the foreseeable election future, the Supreme Court would be packed with Conservative, Republican judges. Justice Kennedy had been a swing vote, a kind of wild card on the court. That time is gone. We live in a new era of a truly Republican court.

The path leading the country to this Republican control, however, was too bumpy to make Republican voters lazy. Had Democrats played friendly and kind, the coming wrath of the Republican voter wouldn't have become so big as we will see in November. With polls being reported as hopeful for Democrats, we could see even more Republicans provoked to vote in 2018 than in 2016. It almost seems as if Democrats and the media are in some kind of secret cooperation to push Republican voters.

With the economy clipping along and so many kept promises from Trump, who has a 50% job approval rating, Republican progress looks likely. There are many states reportedly in play, but that amounts to 44 Senate seats secure for Democrats and 48 secure for Republicans. The reported tossup is a steeper climb for Democrats than Republicans and, with the Kavanaugh turbulence, Republican voters won't be staying home.

In the minds of Democrat voters, a strong Republican court makes them paranoid that Republican police could come to their homes any minute now and burn them alive for flying rainbow flags. This kind of hysteria has been cultivated by Democratic propaganda, though never stated directly, being intended to get Democratic votes, though its effects will be dangerous when those votes aren't enough to win elections.

Republican strategy went correctly. By confirming Kavanaugh, Republicans acted like Republicans, which always brings out the Republican vote. Loss has always brought out Democratic demonstration. While we may be looking at an unusual mid-term victory for the president's party next month, we could also be looking at riots soon after. And, in America just as we see in the swelling #WalkAway movement, the aftermath of riots leads to one thing: repentance.

Cadence of Conflict: Asia, October 8

China's political, socioeconomic worldview is that of a zero-sum game. It has played its socioeconomic game that way for decades. Now, it must empty its reserve coffers to keep its zero-sum game strategy from sinking too fast. This means that it can't use those coffers if a military conflict arose. The United States knows this.

Don't be fooled. The US strategy is to provoke China into a conflict sooner than it wants. In the Western view, China has shown how it will behave by having shown how it has behaved more and more. This is enough to warrant preemptive agitation for the Western taxpayer. In China's view, the world has failed to bestow on China what China deserves; because China rightly deserves what it deserves, China can't lose.

Interpol has now gotten whatever international attention against China's favor that Hong Kong malcontents did not. With the disappearance of Interpol's president into China, whoever didn't care about so-called "Chinese aggression" does now. China's government thinks they sent a message to the world. They did, but the message received is probably not the message that was intended.

As the Pacific conflict escalates, the US-Taiwan aggravation strategy moves into more military cooperation. "Unprecedented" was the word of the week. And, everyone knows what it means just as much as everyone knows why.

Encore of Revival: America, October 15

Trump hosted several guests in the Oval Office this week, including Kanye West, Pastor Andrew Brunson, and Nikki Haley.

Haley is resigning from the United Nations. A likely successor could be Jared Kushner. If Jared is not named her successor, then he will continue to rise in respect behind the scenes elsewhere. Haley mentioned his effective negotiation work with the new NAFTA deal in her resignation.

Andrew Brunson was released from captivity in Turkey relating to imprisonment of Christians in a clash with Middle Eastern religion, law, and culture. His return home was thought to be a lost cause when Trump took office. The president mentioned that North Korea had also been a lost cause by the previous administration, with war being immanent. He pointed out that many supposed "lost causes" had turned around since he took office, Brunson's return being only one of them with many more yet to come.

Inviting Kanye West into the Oval Office gave Kanye a platform to be heard. Apparently he had many things to say that had only been distorted by the media. Being heard from across the desk of the president he supports allowed him to be heard clearly and accurately. He's not the only one with such a need.

Faith Goldy is running for mayor in Toronto. She is surrounded by opposition, including questions about advertising contracts that were not honored and possible lawsuit cases in her favor. She is up against a comfortable incumbent and an establishment comfortable with the incumbent's comfort. Being in the top three candidates she was still rejected from participating in an election debate.

From the look of things, along with the ever-swelling #WalkAway movement, it seems that an election fraud effort may be in effect and over-optimism from the Left is the attempt to persuade public opinion otherwise. Considering that Canada has similar issues, the effort against Trump seems to be part of something both greater and international.

Cadence of Conflict: Asia, October 15

It happened this week. The US finally said outright exactly what Cadence has been saying for years, the strategy in play. According to a Reuters article via Yahoo News, US security adviser John Bolton said, "If they're put back in the proper place they would be if they weren't allowed to steal our technology, their military capabilities would be substantially reduced. And a lot of the tensions we see caused by China would be reduced."

The US wants to put China "back in the proper place". If it weren't for one-sided trade deals over the last to decades and an accumulation of technology that China neither researched, conceptualized, nor paid for, Bolton thinks China would be as friendly as a cute, little house cat, not the bossy tiger it has grown into.

Specifically, the US would need to humble the diesel-powered aircraft carrier, the Liaoning, from which China's other aircraft carriers in the making were reverse-engineered. Taiwan held rehearsals against the Liaoning this week. In other areas, Taiwan isn't backing down, but announced 30 new international flight destinations this week.

Looking at things in this broader context, the escalating military conflict will not result from a trade war gone awry. Rather, the trade war was but a small part of a much larger scheme to provoke China into a military conflict sooner than it wanted. Tech and money has already been cut off. New weapons have been developed and prepared. Now, the US hopes to put China "back in the proper place". In Beijing culture, that means an attempt from the US to shame China on the seas.

We should be preparing for an insulted, post-defeat China and long-term strategists should being their review of the psychological atmosphere in pre-WWII Germany.

Encore of Revival: America, October 22

Saudi leadership is deeply entrenched in an attempt to make the world a better place. Just as Trump has his enemies, so do the Saudis. The Saudi Crowned Prince did not visit Turkey and personally dismember and murder a news reporter, no matter how many anti- fake news activists might have liked him to. There are many alibis in defense of the Saudi royal family, among them that they have many enemies who want violence to continue, who are even willing to engage in violence and blame it on the royal family to stir dissent against the royal family that wants to end violence.

Trump pulled out of the INF treaty, prohibiting medium-range ground-based nukes. Gorbachev doesn't want Trump to pull out, but he hasn't seemed so outspoken about Putin violating the treaty. Trump's defense will be that the treaty has already ended, the US is merely jumping ship from the boat Russia has poked holes in for a long time. Putin's argument is that missile defense in Europe violates attack missile treaties, though that argument needs further explaining before the American public will agree. By having argued that NATO defense violated treaties restricting attack protocols, Putin is more or less acknowledging that he already has a good excuse to violate the INF treaty, but Trump does not. Either way, Russia has nothing to complain about at this point because both parties seem to think the treaty no longer applies.

When your enemy argues that violating a treaty is fair, it's stupid not to pull out of that treaty. Signed documents don't cause missiles to freeze in mid air. Tension between the US rises and lowers based on how much the superpowers want to get along— and signed documents trail after the ebb and flow of the greater tide.

Cadence of Conflict: Asia, October 22

By not labeling China a "currency manipulator", the US is extending an olive branch to Beijing. But, things aren't as they seem. On every level, China is reaching—almost grasping—to save face.

This new artificial moon is honest and runs deep in Chinese culture. As part of being the center of the universe, Chinese culture arguably orbits the moon. The Lunar New Year is celebrated far more, in Chinese culture, than the Western calendar New Year. While the Western press tells of the man-made moon from China as a kind of narcissism, it's genuine and normal interest. The threat is US strategy.

While the US throws olive branch after olive branch, the forest yields other fruit than olives. China is losing money fast. Trump tariffs are gobbling up China's reserves behind the reserves. No matter how friendly China tries to play at this point, the US will continue to deliver one provocation after another until China retaliates with basic human instinct. It won't matter how many "encounter codes" China and the US agree to. The US has decided that China is an enemy and has determined to convince the world as much.

This is not the first military provocation campaign from the US. But, if China wins, it would be a first naval victory for China. Calculate the odds.

Encore of Revival: America, October 29

This past week began rich in fodder for headline minions. Statements like "bomb delivered to home of... [insert prominent Democrat]" and "Kavanaugh recused in three cases..." might convince a non-self-educated idiot that something was wrong. But, anyone who reads past the headlines should know that these stories shouldn't even make the third page.

At least thirteen bombs were delivered, but none of them went off. That's not the work of a "mail bomber", but the work of a "fail bomber" or a "dud mailer". Kavanaugh was recused from the cases because he has already been a judge with a decision and an opinion in those cases. In other words, Kavanaugh was recused for being over-qualified as a judge and being such an honest person that he won't rule a second time on a case he already ruled on in a lower court.

Initially, the mailed duds looked like typical Democratic "wolf" crying. After the Ford testimony theater and unreported proof that another Kavanaugh accusation wasn't true, Americans suspected the mail duds were also a self-inflicted conspiracy for pre-election sympathy. But, as more and more high profile Democratic heavyweights received dud bomb packages, it seemed more like an unexpected ruse that the Democratic media machine was hoping to salvage.

Then, terror struck. For the Democratic media machine, this meant losing valuable headline space before an election. For Jewish families in Pittsburgh, it meant grief and loss.

Then, the caravan halted. Mexico offered refugee lifestyle—housing, employment, education—a few even applied, making the caravan smaller. A child was kidnapped and the caravan stopped moving.

Midweek, the usual headline fodder took a 110° jackknife turn. What happened?—A shot across the bow happened, from whom we just don't know.

Whatever story lays behind this "fail dud bomber", this week was a warning to Democrats at the highest levels. Whether this was a self-inflicted media stunt that failed to get whatever victim election favor status was hoped for or if it was a genuine surprise, Democrats no longer have power. Their caravan can't move on schedule. They aren't as popular as they once thought. And, most sacred to Democratic elite class party bosses, their home addresses are known to scary people. If that's not a shot across their bow, nothing is.

Cadence of Conflict: Asia, October 29

The Pacific Ocean has become a chess board of moving pawns, castling kings, bluffs, and propaganda. China offers the moon to small countries, the US warns that no "free" gift comes without strings attached. When Trump pulled out of the INF treaty for supposed Russian violations, Russia went on high alert at home and called it "preparing for war". Russia being ready for war means China feeling more confident about busting a move.

Given regional instability, Japan and India are talking big. They want cooperative military exercises. They will also need passage through that section of the ocean—the South Sea—that China drew a nine-dash line around. America won't be the only challenger to China's new notion of "ocean ownership". As China gets more and more assertive, even the British are on edge. Nothing happens in the Western Pacific unnoticed.

Is China strong enough to win a military conflict? A Chinese rocket failed at launch. In the news, it's reported as a "private company", but there is no such thing in China, by Western understanding of a "private company" anyhow. The reason it failed is probably rooted in the sister controversy to trade: reverse engineering and technology copying. China couldn't launch the rocket, in all likelihood, because too much of the technology used by China wasn't invented by China, but invented by someone else, made in China, and copied by China—but not understood by China. Such is the tech of this "private company" and the tech that made China so big as it is today and the tech it would use in battle. Russia would be wise to not depend on that tech. And, small countries would be wise to remember that the "great China" was made great by a tilted-trade, copied-tech cash cow that is no longer making milk.

China's National Tourism Administration suspended group tours to one of China's many coveted destinations in Taiwan. The delay is scheduled to last from early November into April. November is an election month for both the US and Taiwan. It's a big month for expos in Taiwan, especially a flora expo in the city where tours were suspended, Taichung. November is also when a large group from the US Navy will make a show of force near China's man-made islands.

Encore of Revival: America, November 5

Doom and gloom flood the media on the eve of Trump's first midterm election. Americans come off the weekend onto a big, info-flooded, single day of business and news before voting on Tuesday. Will the country gain momentum after the sharp turn it took two years ago or will it do a 170° and head almost back to where it was going under Obama?

Polls and forecasts spelled constant doom for the Republican party these past few months, all while Trump pulls farther and farther ahead in presidential polls. Too many so-called "experts" in mass media predict failure for Conservatives no matter what the outcome will be. With the immature display from Democrats during the Kavanaugh hearings, compounded with the growing #WalkAway movement, Conservatives have become so victimized and energized that it's hard to imagine Republicans not gaining seats in both the House and Senate. A loss would beg questions of meddling.

Ironically, this election will decide more about the mainstream news media than it will about the nation. A Republican agenda over the next six years is more foreseeable than the media would have the nation believe. But, less clear is how much faith voters will maintain in the media. No matter what party a voter casts a ballot for, news networks that are as wrong they have been the past three years should not be able to stay in business. While voters will likely choose Republicans two elections in a row, viewers—Democratic and Republican alike—will likely choose to keep watching news networks that were wrong about Republicans two elections in a row.

Considering the fact that news networks stay in business with how wrong they were in predicting Trump's 2016 loss, it's a miracle any of them are still in business, let alone if they are wrong again in 2018. This miracle of such inaccurate news networks staying in business for so long is a big enough miracle to make the most avid Atheist believe in God.

Cadence of Conflict: Asia, November 5

China is less and less popular in the news. It's almost conspiracy-like—how much negative news comes out against China in the Western press at once.

The Trump administration backs Micron with legal action against Fujian Jinhua, an American company vs a Chinese company, over tech theft. At the same time, Jeff Sessions suddenly decides to appear in front of cameras and decry China for cyberspying on the US—a completely unrelated matter except that it is bad press for China. Then, the Taipei Times runs a front page story on illegal Chinese crabs being imported, but not passing a health inspection, with involved companies given a hefty fine, while pushing a North Korean nuke "restart" story to page five! The Taipei Times ran another front page story of China creating fake social media accounts to meddle in Taiwan's upcoming midterm election.

The truthfulness of this flood of anti-China news is not as important as its timing and priority among headlines. Popular sentiment is more powerful than missiles in a conflict between nations. On that front, the West has already won. Don't think for a moment that missiles won't follow to secure

what the war of words already won by a deck
stacked in the news.

Encore of Revival: America, November 12

This was an astonishing victory for Republicans for any year, especially a controlling party midterm. Senate Republicans have rarely held this many seats since the FDR days except Reagan and W Bush. Losses in the House were among the lowest losses for a controlling party midterm. By gaining seats in the Senate, Republicans are winning the long game. We are headed for a possible supermajority by the end of Trump's second term. In the next two years, House Democrats will have just enough power to be irritating, but not enough to make any difference, other than helping Trump get re-elected in 2020.

Democrats are darned if they do and darned if they don't. Trump's appointees can be approved faster and impeachment in the House would die in the Senate. Opposition party power is good for presidential elections. Trump's best course of action would be to deliver the strongest Conservative proposals so Democrats can go on record as obstructionists. The best course of action for Democrats would be to talk and vote like Republicans, which has always been historically favorable, proven with Democratic Rahm Emanuel -led "blue dog" victory in 2006.

Results are still being counted. At last count, Democrats gained 30 seats in the House and had control of the House by 7. Most of those states had Democratic Senate and gubernatorial victories. In this victory for Democrats, nothing seems out of the ordinary. The election results appear to be real and fair; Democrats won the House fair and square.

The question of some after-election counting and recounting, however, seems sketchy. The Arizona Senate race looks like a lost cause for the Republican candidate. Arguably from Senate voting records, the Arizona seat up for grabs was not gained by Democrats except in name only. That Senate seat will be up the election Trump leaves office. But, that's a different story from a cluster of recount fiascos in Florida and Georgia, where recounting is a matter of procedure, not questionable results. The losers in those elections are pushing in hopes that close results can easily be tipped. If recounts were to change those results, that would open bigger questions, bigger objections, and bigger investigations. So far, the number of ballots in question would not change the results; miscounts would.

Even with the ground Republicans took, Democrats outspent Republicans by roughly $300M. Ironically, Democrats campaign on a platform of opposing big money and suspect business man Trump of trying to buy the presidency. The spending was bad optics for them.

Trump's proved helpful on the campaign trail.
Many Republicans who pushed him away lost.
Senate Republicans defeated incumbents in
Florida, Indiana, Missouri, and North Dakota.
Senate Republicans also held vacant seats in
Tennessee and Utah. 26 Republicans retired, more
than any midterm year since 1974, the greatest
retirements being 27 in 2008.

FDR holds both the greatest midterm gain and
midterm loss since his time as president. After
FDR, the greatest midterm loss was Obama's first
midterm. The greatest midterm gain in the Senate
was Trump, the second-greatest being JFK with
+3. This was a favorable midterm year for
Republicans. But, already you read that right here
at Pacific Daily Times before the election. So, while
Republicans had a historic election, Pacific Daily
Times has set a new standard for accuracy in the
media.

Cadence of Conflict: Asia, November 12

Xi Jinping announced yet another new policy for China: Blaming other countries is wrong, each country must deal with its own economic and environmental issues without the problem being someone else's fault. While this 180° new direction should be welcoming to foreign companies whose intellectual property was taken by China, along with the neighboring lands that China has no presence in, yet threatened to invade, such as Taiwan, Xi gave no particular details as to how he planned to adjust China's current action plan. In fact, Xi's announcement came as if it was not any change at all, but a continuation of the current policy, that taking unoccupied territory and accumulating foreign technology without payment was necessary for China's economic and environmental well being within its borders. Perhaps his intention was to further confuse the West about China's international policy or perhaps he has made himself even more understandable than he ever has before. We'll have to wait and see what actions follow to interpret Xi's meaning.

China is growing its ties with Israel, for the time being. An infrastructure deal is said to be the kind that will irritate US President Trump. China, however, should be more concerned. Israel has some of the best counter-intel gathering in the world. If China does use the building contracts as an opportunity to spy, after Israel has a chance to respond, it might be the Chinese who break contract. Israel is one nation that China won't be able to bully. As stubborn as ancient Asian worldviews can still be today, Israeli culture can be more stubborn. It's not about race, it's about two cultures about to collide. 'Tis folly to double-cross a nation whose name means "wrestles with God"; and the name is not a reference to wrestling with China.

This week, Taiwan and Hong Kong did what they do best more than they have done before. When a Financial Times writer is banned from Hong Kong because he intends to interview an author—and that author's speaking engagements are shut down after Chinese requests—the wisdom of Roger Branigin returns to the western readership: "I never argue with a man who buys ink by the barrel." China wasn't satisfied to argue with an author who is more famous for it, but now wants to argue with more in the ink business. But, that wasn't the most significant development of the week. Taiwan is labeled as the "island of hope" for Asia at an international forum for Human Rights hosted in Taipei.

Encore of Revival: America, November 19

John Kelly's failure to book seats for the first lady
on Airforce One, thereby creating security snafus
and other logistic problems, was no mere oversight.
A military man made White House chief of staff
doesn't make security-logistic mistakes. Getting
along with the first lady personally, then giving her
a smaller staff than previous first ladies, refusing
to promote her staff while promoting his own—all
these were indications of something deeper.

Pacific Daily Times' Symphony suggested on
September 10 that the "mole" who wrote the
infamous, and since forgotten, "New York Times
essay" fit the profile of someone like John Kelly.
The clashes leading up to his rumored replacement
fit the profile even more. Similarly, is a DHS chief
performing poorly—another non-accident—, then
Kelly clashing with security adviser John Bolton
when Bolton criticized the poor performance. Try
this hypothetical scenario: The essay author was in
cahoots with other saboteurs; when a fellow
saboteur was called-out, the saboteur naturally got
defensive. Such a saboteur probably didn't storm
out of the White House on October 18 from mere
rage, but to perform apparently-needed damage
control since his plans for sabotage were at risk.
That scenario may not be true, but it would explain
a lot. Does it seem all that strange that Kelly and

the DHS chief he was so defensive of would both be on the radar for replacement?

Theories to fit the pieces together, however, are no more than theories. All we know from here is that a theory made Kelly's departure all too predictable and that, to know the rest, we'll just have to wait and see. Replacing a cabinet member should be easier with Governor Rick Scott having secured the fifty-second Republican seat in the Senate.

With rules of conduct in place for the White House press, it will be easier for reporters to have fair access to questions and easier for the White House to kick out reporters who want to take mic time from others. For suing the woman who worked at the White House who tried to take away the White House microphone from Jim Acosta—on camera—with no injury—when he wouldn't yield the floor to his peers—CNN and Acosta should be ashamed.

Cadence of Conflict: Asia, November 19

In Taiwanese politics, a mayor candidate's comments about his own benefits from drinking honey-lemonade sparked retribution from the medical community. After a lump under his eye went away, apparently from a vegetarian and honey-lemonade diet, he actually said so. A professional from a hospital was quick to weigh in. It's understandable. If people learned that honey could cure disease, hospital profits would plunge. More importantly, Taiwanese political debates would become outright boring without the ability to, as the saying goes, make lemonade from political debates.

But, lemonade really is important. Google search results even saw a spike after this essential talk of Taiwanese politics made news.

Meanwhile, at the ASEAN summit in Singapore, Prime Minister Lee Hsien Loong called for nations to come together at a time when Southeast Asian stability was under threat. In anticipation of APEC after ASEAN, Mike Pence started talking tough, wanting results and genuine action from China concerning an even-flow of trade. He elaborated, that the US has a quarter of a billion dollars in tariffs and isn't afraid to go twice as high as well as take more "diplomatic" action. It was a strong "they

know that we know that they know what we think"
remark, the kind that precedes otherwise
objectionable action to make the action
unobjectionable.

Later, at APEC, Pence warned of returning to a
"cold war" while making plans for a US-Australian
naval base in Papua New Guinea. Rather than
dropping its tilted tariffs on goods, China has been
openly gearing up for all out war three weeks.
APEC ended without a written agreement between
member nations for the first time ever because of
the disagreements between the US and China.

This past weekend, Taiwan did something that
China despises every bit as much as it cannot
identify with: Taiwan hosted democratic election
campaigns. With all the strong rhetoric concerning
Taiwan, independence, and China's loudly and
often-spoken determination to invade Taiwan, there
shouldn't be any question where China's war-in-
preparation will start and why America will easily
get involved.

America is already involved in Taiwan to quite an
extent. AIT, the unofficial yet de facto US embassy
in Taiwan, had an interview scheduled for release
with a large TV network in Taiwan. But, after the
interview, the TV network, TVBS, scrapped the
interview. So, AIT shared the interview in its
Facebook page, rather than relying on TVBS.

With the history lessons about Taiwan in almost
every Taiwan-related story in the Western press,
Americans will take an advancement against

Taiwan as an advancement against themselves. China would be perceived as an aggressor and rightly so. Everything the US has done to provoke and irritate China would have only worked if China possessed the old school "Asian Pride" that Sun Tzu warned against, a pride that can't be permitted in a world's superpower because such pride is easily provoked just as much as it is easily shattered. Hardened pride makes for brittle peace. That's something that the entire West won't allow, the US notwithstanding.

Encore of Revival: America, November 26

The US faces politics within and without. President Trump refers to judges appointed by a president; Chief Justice Roberts rebuts, effectively, that judges aren't owned by presidents. Trump never said they were, he was referring to who appointed them. Who makes an appointment is relevant, even in a court trial. Unless the question, "Who appointed you?" has never been answered by a plaintiff or witness in court, Roberts misunderstood. It would be best that the chief justice accurately understand the commander-in-chief's "original intent". As for Roberts's claim that courts are impartial, that certainly is what we all hope for. Trump's predication is that perfection is a humanly unreachable destination, which is why we need courts in the first place.

At the border, Mexico allowed the so-named "caravan", now reported at over 8k people, to march through its country seeking immediate help, instant protection, urgent safety, emergency respite from political persecution—or some other timely need that is required to receive "asylum". Asylum is not a fun thing to receive and often means never being allowed to leave the country once inside. Edward Snowden wasn't allowed to walk from Hong Kong to Moscow, picking and choosing which country he could seek asylum from; he had to get it right where he was, before leaving the international terminal. If anyone in that caravan can prove that the kinds of protection an asylum specifically grants could not be provided by the many countries they marched through for many weeks, then they should be granted an asylum. They would also need to prove that they would never return to their home country to visit family, no matter what. That's a tall order. But, if they can do it, they deserve it, but only if.

The Russianewsgategate scandal scandal is still barking and honking, predicting drama and awe, while quietly reminding audiences that there will probably be no indictment. 'Tis no more than theater at this point, but an act that needs to be kept up so that the cast won't be accused of having been pretending the whole time. After Kavanaugh's unfair trial dubbed a "hearing", avoiding the appearance of fakery in DC theater is important these days.

Whatever is going on in the US is a lot better than what's going on in Europe. We are witnessing ancient, Biblical prophecy fulfilled in our day: The winged lion of Daniel 7:4 had the eagle's wings removed and has now been given the sane mind of a human. While eagle's wings internationally represent America's mascot, the lion represents Britain's. While Prime Minister May gave her speech about the Brexit status, she stood behind the crest of Britain's lion. It is clear from her speech—by leaving the EU, Britain is no longer part of the madness festering in Europe.

Cadence of Conflict: Asia, November 26

Taiwan held something akin to a "mid-term" election this past Saturday. The people revolted against the previous revolt. When electing the DPP two years ago, the people were fed up with the capitulation policies of Ma. Now, they are fed up with bad management of infrastructure, also an "establishment culture" surfacing in what should be the "opposition party", among other grievances. Taiwan's government cautioned China to wait and see how the election affects cross-strait policy before jumping to any conclusions—because they think China can't figure that out.

China's government and the Western press are going head to head. China held the American children of an estranged father and money laundering defendant. The New York Times made sure to plaster the picture of the young adult brother and sister at the top of the story. Exploiting children to sway outcomes just isn't fair.

But, it didn't stop at children. The New York Times also posted about cheap labor building Chinese AI. And, Forbes published an article with a graph that makes it look like China's economy has bottomed out. The battle between China and its great and powerful foe—the Western press—rages on. China

is at an unfair disadvantage, but presses forward
fearlessly and valiantly.

Encore of Revival: America, December 3

Former President George Herbert Walker Bush, the 41st president, is dead at 94.

While the Bush family and the nation mourn, politics continue as usual.

The "Mark Meadows Plan" for Congressional Republicans foreshadows political posturing of the next two years: Democrats will be a powerless foil supporting the re-election of Trump. Just how Democrats harassed the Regan administration with the Olly North investigations, harassed Supreme Justices Kavanaugh and Thomas with sexual harassment allegations—just how the House Republicans harassed Clinton with the Kenneth Star -led investigation—so will this Democratic House irritate the electorate over the next two years. Even if the House impeaches the president as it did Clinton, there isn't foreseeable traction in the 52-seat strong Republican Senate.

The latest "shock and faux" campaign from the press attempts to scare readers with the notion that Russia did not exercise leverage over Trump— but they could have—because Trump decided not to build a project in Russia that everyone knew about him not building when he would have been allowed to build it anyway. The reason, as this latest "wow" campaign goes, is because Trump is now reported to be the center of the Mueller investigation. Really? That's news?

The next two years will be as entertaining as watching a cat who thinks it's a god, but just can't figure out why it can't get anyone to obey.

Cadence of Conflict: Asia, December 3

Taiwan President Tsai Ing-Wen apologizing after a mid-term defeat at the provincial level will not demonstrate strength on her part, but she shows respect and stability in maintaining her appointees and policy toward China. Having not stood her ground on information about proposal that would have set Taiwan's team name at the Olympics in Japan as "Taiwan", instead of "Taipei", she lost important support from the Formosan Association for Public Affairs, a group that seeks to have Taiwan internationally recognized as an independent nation.

Taiwan's premier, William Lai, does stand for Taiwanese independence, held remarkable popularity in his reelection as mayor, and is the shoe-in candidate if he were to run in 2020 instead of Tsai. Tsai's re-election is uncertain. What happens will depend on Taiwanese politics, which are too adolescent to not be surprised by. Main matters at stake include Taiwan developing faster responses to correct disinformation given to the public and a focus on better quality with internal governance and infrastructure. Interestingly, information and governance—not China itself—are at the heart of resistance to China.

If Taiwan declares independence from China, or takes too many steps to join international bodies like the UN, as Beijing has stated, we could be looking at all out war. Some in the political "news-o-sphere" call Taiwan a "flashpoint". China hangs onto hopes of retaking Taiwan like King John's suicidal siege of Rochester Castle. All the US does is provoke.

The latest provocation came late last week when Japan opened the path to retrofitting "helicopter carriers" into fixed-wing aircraft carriers. Japan looks to acquire 142 F35s—42 As and now 100 Bs; the UK eyes 138, about half of them to go to the Royal Navy. There are too many high-tech American aircraft in China's backyard for China's comfort. And, the US did two more sail-bys—one near China's man-made islands, the other through the Taiwan Strait. China lobbed another "demarche" protest with Washington, presuming the action to be "provocative".

Then came the US-China 90 day cease fire between Trump and Xi at the G20 this past weekend. A lot can happen in 90 days, whether politically, economically, or militarily.

Encore of Revival: America, December 10

The theory presented on September 10 and November 19 proved useful enough to predict White House Chief of Staff John Kelly's departure. No one announces in advance that someone is leaving—before the departure, without also announcing a replacement. Nobody cares about a boss whose boss already announced would be leaving. That's how to cripple any malevolent powers of an administrator that can't be quickly unplugged, but needs to go—and do so without raising suspicion that the administrator did anything wrong. Even in his dismissal—not a "retirement"—Kelly fits the bill as the author of the "New York Times essay", right down to getting tossed out in a way that no one would suspect a darned thing.

France is in trouble. The president who snubbed Trump has fallen into disfavor with his own people. This largely comes down to grandiose promises made by socialist agendas that everyone should have known could not deliver because of foresight rooted in hindsight. Socialism never delivers anything but what we see in France now. As for ado about Brexit, there's no point in worrying so much since the queen can decide anyway, if she wants to. That's what the British always tell Americans is so wonderful about the UK's constitutional monarchy. But, acting like this is a problem helps keep the British press afloat.

A Trump campaign payment is now being compared to a situation with 2004 Democratic candidate John Edwards. But, that has three major holes in its boat: 1. The accusation encircles alleged campaign finance violations surrounding the Trump organization's lawyer, Cohen, whose job it was to give legal advice; Trump is not a lawyer, Edwards was. Can a lawyer be witness against the client he advised, or secretly recorded? 2. The Mueller investigation sought to understand whether there was wrongful involvement with Russia and Trump. The Fourth Amendment limits the scope of search and seizure to a probable cause and any seized items must be specified by the warrant in advance. By starting with an investigation between Trump and Russia, but ending with a campaign finance accusation against a candidate accused by the lawyer who advised him, this has gone well beyond the scope that the Fourth Amendment was intended to limit. If courts allow this, it shows how much our legal justice system has wandered from the Constitution. 3. The electorate will want a good explanation for why Hillary wasn't treated this way. The best reason so far would be that the courts have been usurped as a cudgel for political rivals. It's not Trump who needs to be worried about an indictment; it's the legal justice system itself that is about to go on trial.

Cadence of Conflict: Asia, December 10

The "Huawei arrest" sends yet another a irritatingly mixed message to China. China believes that a "strong response" concerning Taiwan will convince the US to back away from support for Taiwan. Conveniently for China, the recent provincial elections in Taiwan seem encouraging and Beijing has reached out to Taiwanese cities that just elected pro-Beijing party candidates.

Premier William Lai intends to resign at the "right time". Could that time be what is necessary so he can run for president? Taiwanese politics are quite unpredictable. All we should expect is a series of surprises before, during, and after 2020. Considering where things stand in the world, we must remember that there is no way the UK could be on Taiwan's side, especially since the UK has concerns about Taiwanese fisherman illegally killing dolphins as shark bait. With opportunity seeming to open, and the increased possibility of the loud-spoken, pro-independence William Lai to run for office, Beijing may be feeling put in an ever tightening situation that compels action.

As concerned as the Chinese are about security, they are far more concerned about insult. Without any sympathy from Western news audiences, an extradition of the Huawei executive from Canada to

the US could push China over the edge. China
believes that its horrific past justifies its conduct
today. It is only a matter of time before Beijing
decides that a strike against Taiwan, supported by
cooperation with Taiwanese city governments,
would send the US out of the region. Taiwan may
not be seen by Beijing as the irritant of tensions,
but the solution to them. The US might have a
different opinion.

Encore of Revival, America, December 17

Every accusation against Trump so far sets a precedent to indite James Comey for refusing to prosecute Hillary for worse crimes. Trump's actual crime was unwritten, that he threatened the comfortable cash cow machine run by a parasitic establishment accurately referred to as "the swamp". These increasingly petty, evermore numerous, and parabolically dramatic accusations will not end in turning votes against Trump, but toward him. The only turnings against will be the masses revolting against the establishment for its attacks against Trump and a revolt against the media that reports the attacks as "fair". The public will see this as quite unfair because of greater priorities going unmentioned, including a multi-million dollar hush-slush fund in Congress.

So, the swamp's machine attacked a dirty lawyer and sentenced him to prison. Now, that lawyer has suddenly turned to saint because he wants to get out of jail by speaking against his own client—a president hated by the same swamp. Can a lawyer that the DOJ has worked so hard to imprison as a sleeze bag suddenly be deemed a credible witness without any ill motives? Connect the dots. The swamp always wants everything both ways.

The swamp is indeed ramping up the assault against Trump, but not because of any new position of strength; the swamp is on attack because the swamp is desperate. What we're about to see in the next two years will be Kavanaugh all over again, only this time it will push Trump to re-election, better than before.

Then we have the Brexitexit. Questions needs to be asked about what connections nay-voters in Parliament have to Brussels. British politics work differently from American. Prime Minister Chamberlain allowed Hitler to rise in power while Parliament kept Winston away. Once the feckless mess grew intolerable, the king had to intervene. After Winston won the war—with the help of some extremely profitable former colonies in America that the Britons claim they carelessly misplaced—the Britons ousted Winston after his warnings that Russia was a rising danger. No doubt many in Great Britain will forget their frustration with past attempts to unite Europe, or the recent attempt—the EU—in squandering British tax dollars on socialist promises to solve self-made problems, such as more recently seen in France.

One of the few wise prime ministers, Margret Thatcher, said, "The trouble with Socialism is that eventually you run out of other people's money." Now, the EU has run out of the Britons' money and "will allow" the Britons to stay in if they want—and some Britons are actually talking about staying in. The American way—which defeated the Nazis for the British—would be for British Parliament to pass its own terms first, giving the EU the ultimatum. If May wants to keep her job, she should tell Parliament, "Give me whatever terms you accept, then I will defend them before Brussels." But, that would require the strong spine of a cowgirl, not the tender skin of true gentlemen. There are many smart people in Great Britain, just not any that we can see from the decisions being made right now.

The way things look, America will need to come to the rescue of our British brothers yet again. Given America's improving situation, it looks like we'll be able.

Cadence of Conflict: Asia, December 17

While China would attempt to send the US out of its backyard by shocking the US with an invasion of Taiwan, that motive in itself would not be enough to push China to war. Beijing believes that controlling more territory is the solution to current problems with its own territory. In urban terms, it would be like believing the reason you have problems in your home is because you don't own the home nextdoor—you deserve to own it, after all; so take it, "by force if necessary." That part of Chinese culture—needing to occupy more surroundings in order to solve problems at home, rather than after solving problems at home—is the part of the Beijing mindset that will actually push China to invade. The time of the invasion will come when Beijing believes that solving its problems at home—specifically with Western press and free speech—can wait no longer. Then, China will invade Taiwan while genuinely believing that all of China's problems within its current borders will thus vanish over night.

But, the US doesn't think the way Beijing thinks the US thinks. While many Americans will be surprised by China's invasion of Taiwan, Beijing will be surprised even more by the American electorate's response to support recompense against China.

In Chinese media, a Chinese Air Force colonel's recommendation that PLA Navy ships ram US Navy ships is not an actual recommendation for strategy as much as it is an attempt at repulsive rhetoric. Chinese culture presumes that a public suggestion is an indirect warning with no intention of follow-through, and because it has no intention of follow-through, it is therefore a "powerful-polite" way of attempting to tell the US to leave. That is how cultural, indirect communication with the Chinese works. Though it is possible that the Chinese might become enraged enough to follow this action by ramming US ships at sea, it would take less rage for China to decide to invade Taiwan. From Beijing's view, unlike retaking the well-deserved Taiwan, ramming a US ship would be an actual assault. If the Chinese-American war begins with a rammed ship, that would indicate a very angry China.

Encore of Revival: America, December 24

The government shutdown is good for Trump and good for the wall. He said what he meant and he meant he wasn't bluffing. Good, old fashion follow-through is one of DC's lost virtues. If the current budget isn't passed by the start of the new 116th Congress on January 3, then it will die. It already has approval of the White House and has passed the House. The quickest way to end the government shutdown is for the Senate to pass the bill.

Ultimately this is a game of "chicken". Either way, we should expect whining everyday. The key to Congress surviving a government shutdown is the theater of talking everyday as if "today's the day" that the government will reopen. It's somewhat akin to the act that Democrats and drive-by news anchors put on about how "today's the day" when they will find the "silver bullet" to stop Trump.

There is no such silver bullet, not even today.

The main actors rising above the dust are the Kushners. Jared and Ivanka are drafting deals and growing coalitions, no matter their father's opponents. Their progress should be bigger news.

So, over Christmas, the worms of Capitol Hill take pot shots at each other and the president is referred to as a child for sticking to his promises, just as Clinton did when he vetoed the budget. One of the best kept secrets about government shutdowns is that the government doesn't actually shut down. To some, that's a disappointment. Even Mueller's investigation continues, but the Supreme Court might stuff coal in his stocking. The holiday season has many more surprises yet to come.

Cadence of Conflict: Asia, December 24

China detains two Canadians with remark and in the wake of a single Huawei executive's arrest. Given the surfacing connections the executive's family had to Mao, China likely views the value of arrested people as equally balanced; the West merely views China as having committed three criminal acts.

Huawei has gotten into more and more trouble the more it has been in the spotlight. Now, Europe even has its doubts. China's sources of money and influences are drying up more and more.

But, an opinion article from Bloomberg invariably proves that some car makers managed to keep their technology out of the hands of China—mainly by keeping it out of China until it was out of date. Moreover, China has made proposals within its government to allow foreign companies to keep their technology secret. So, that should end any and every doubt about what a wonderful place China is for any and all manufacturing.

On the military side, China is announcing that it is finally pursuing the same quiet submarine technologies that the US, Russia, and India are also pursuing. So, that's it. The West should give up because, after all, China is going to win.

The US, however, is in a different position. If China were to initiate a conflict with the US, say by attempting to assert control over Taiwan "by force if necessary", China might not get as much help from its rumored spy partner, Russia. Taiwan is unlike Crimea, which held a referendum with overwhelming favor to return to Russia. And, with the US out of Russian-interested territories, like Syria and Afghanistan, there is little Russia would have to object to in the US following its own law to defend Taiwan, already on the books. A recessed Congress is certainly willing.

Encore of Revival: America, December 31

Jerome Corsi is after the FBI family for going after him and his family. Mueller wanted to delay the hearing of Corsi's lawsuit against the FBI, basically arguing that the shutdown had shutdown his investigation—except that it hasn't. Trump stayed in Washington over the holiday shutdown, missing his family in Florida, while Nanci Pelosi and Maxine Waters went on vacation in Hawaii and the Bahamas, respectively—and they say Trump doesn't understand politics. The stock market was said to be in the tank, and it was "all Trump's fault"—until it it wasn't either anymore.

The biggest news—of things that actually happened "new"—was Kevin Spacey. Apparently Underwood is back from the dead. The character assassination machine has systematically picked off anyone in the national spotlight who didn't step in line—until that didn't work against Trump— then, it simply didn't work. But, now that it's going up against one of the few actual actors in Hollywood—Spacey—along with Conservatives like Jerome Corsi and Dennis Prager, that machine itself might just blow a transformer and light up the national sky more than Con Edison lit up New York.

It looks like Kevin Spacy is about to "Underwood" Hollywood, and that will only be the beginning.

Merry Christmas and Happy New Year!

Cadence of Conflict: Asia, December 31

China and the US—more specifically Xi and Trump—are talking more and more about talking more and more about trade. China has drafted legislation to propose making China a fair country to outsiders. What a great proposed Christmas gift, just before the New Year.

In light of everything, China seems to be making other concessions to US demands. But, one issue lingers in the back-of-the-room shadows: Taiwan. The US is bound by near-treaty to defend Taiwan if China were to invade. And, Taiwan just keeps taking pot shots. And, China doesn't seem to notice the conflict on the US side of the talks.

###

About the Author

Jesse Steele is an American writer in Asia who wears many hats. He learned piano as a kid, studied Bible in college, and currently does podcasting, web contenting, cloud control, and brand design. He likes golf, water, speed, music, kung fu, art, and stories.

Jesse owns various brands, occasionally teaches writing and piano, and preaches the evangels of Linux, Open-Source, and Jesus.

Poetry is code.™

books@jessesteele.com
books.jessesteele.com